**Think
Through
History**

Minds and Machines

Britain 1750-1900

Authors:

Jamie Byrom

Christine Counsell

Michael Gorman

Michael Riley

Andrew Wrenn

LONGMAN

Minds and Machines – Britain 1750–1900

The making of money

The making of masters

George III 1760-1820

George IV 1820-1830

1766 James Watt improved the steam engine

1784 Styal Mill built

1787 Anti Slavery Society formed

1789 French Revolution began

1815 Battle of Waterloo

1819 Peterloo Massacre

The making of minds

William IV
1830-1837

Victoria
1837-1901

1831 First cholera outbreak

1832 'Great' Reform Act

1834 New Poor Law

1845 Irish famine

1847 10 Hour Factory Act

1848 Chartist movement failed

1857 Indian 'Mutiny'

1859 Darwin's 'Origin of Species'

1867 2nd Reform Act

1875 Public Health Act

1881 Repeal of the Contagious Diseases Act

1897 Diamond Jubilee celebrations

All change

Why were so many people on the move between 1750 and 1900?

1

Think

- Do you think that this painting shows the town or the countryside?

- What details in the painting help you to make your choice?

A painting by William W. Morris, 1852

Believe it or not, the picture opposite shows a scene from a large city. If you thought that the picture showed the countryside you were being perfectly sensible. After all, the picture shows trees, grass and a cow! It certainly seems like an odd scene for the middle of a city.

The picture was painted in 1852. It shows a milk stall set up in a part of St James's Park in London. It might seem strange to us, but this was a common sight in many large towns and cities. It reminds us of the big problem faced by all towns. How were the towns to get food?

People in towns needed fresh milk and other foodstuffs from the countryside. Country people had always travelled into towns and cities to sell their goods. Sometimes, as in this picture, cows were kept on common land and other open spaces in the city. Cattle were not an uncommon sight in London. Large herds of cattle had long been driven to the great market at Smithfield.

Huge changes took place between 1750 and 1900. In 1850, some towns and cities were ten times as big as they had been 100 years before. Producing enough food for all these people and getting food from countryside to town was now a very big operation.

The growth of towns was part of the enormous change that historians call the **Industrial Revolution**. At that time people were on the move more than ever before. Large numbers of people moved from countryside to town. Large numbers of people travelled very long distances to other countries never to return. There were also new methods of transport, allowing people and goods to travel faster than ever before. Even the people who did not move at all were affected by other people who did! Their work, ideas and standard of living were all affected by these and many other changes.

Your enquiry

In this enquiry you will gain an overview of just one of the changes that took place between 1750 and 1900 – the movement of people. You will build up an outline picture of **where** and **why** people moved. You will also discover **how** people moved from place to place. At the end of the enquiry you will work out how these changes were linked to the many other big changes that took place during an astonishing 150 years of change. You will make diagrams to show how all these changes link up.

From country to town

By 1900 there were nearly five times as many people in Britain as there were in 1750. These figures show how and when the population of the British Isles grew.

Year	England	Wales	Scotland	Ireland	Total
1701	5,100,000	450,000	1,000,000	2,700,000	9,250,000
1751	5,800,000	500,000	1,200,000	3,200,000	10,700,000
1801	8,700,000	600,000	1,600,000	5,000,000	15,900,000
1851	16,800,000	1,200,000	2,900,000	6,500,000	27,400,000
1871	21,300,000	1,400,000	3,400,000	5,400,000	31,500,000
1901	30,500,000	2,000,000	4,500,000	4,500,000	41,500,000

Think

- Which of the four parts of the British Isles increased its population by six times between 1701 and 1901?

- Which country had a population of two million in 1901?

- Which country experienced a fall in its population between 1801 and 1901?

At the same time as this big population increase, there was a move from the countryside to the towns. The fast-developing iron, coal and textile industries were creating new work. The workers in these new industries needed somewhere to live. For example, between 1750 and 1800 the population of Manchester increased from 18,000 to 90,000 people.

These four piecharts show the changes in the balance of population between towns and countryside in Britain.

1801
Urban 31%
Rural 69%

1841
Urban 46%
Rural 54%

1851
Urban 50%
Rural 50%

1881
Urban 68%
Rural 32%

Think

- Look carefully at the piecharts. What do **rural** and **urban** mean?

- In what year was the population in the towns and the population in the countryside roughly the same?

The rise in population and the move to the cities led to some other big changes. Here are two of these changes:

1   There was a rise in the demand for food and for factory goods. People in the towns and cities did not make their own food and clothes in the way that country people did. The move to the cities encouraged people to spend more money in the shops.

2   Completely new communities developed. For example, the growth of the coal and iron industry led to thousands of new jobs in the western lowlands of Scotland. This was why the population of Glasgow rose from 77,000 in 1800 to 904,000 by 1900.

You are going to make a set of Change Cards about demographic change. Demographic changes are changes to do with <u>population</u> growth and movement. Make two little cards like these below.

On your first card sum up what happened to the population in Britain between 1750 and 1900. On your second card describe how the population moved from countryside to town. Write no more than two sentences on each card. Write in large, bold print (or use a computer).

Design a little symbol for both of your cards. Your symbol should show that the cards are about demographic change. For example, you could use a little piechart, tiny symbols for town and country, or perhaps a map.

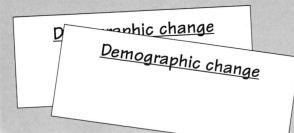

Demographic change

'For I was tired of England Sir'

The population did not only move from town to country.
The people on this ship would probably never see their families
and friends again. They are leaving to go to another continent.

'The Emigrant Ship' by Charles Staniland

In the 19th century millions of Europeans left home and started life in another country. Nearly twelve million people left Britain, either for the United States of America or for parts of the British Empire. This map shows you the places where most British **emigrants** went.

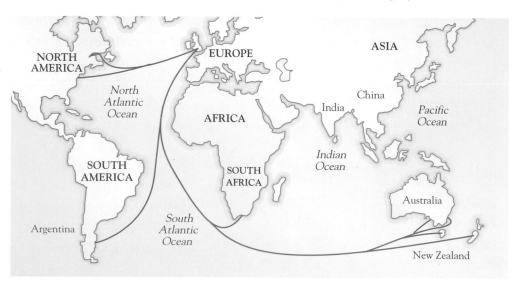

Where British emigrants went in the nineteenth century

8

Most of the emigrants left because of hardship. The numbers of people leaving Britain increased rapidly during the 1830s and 1840s. During these years many working people suffered terrible difficulties caused by low wages or unemployment and high bread prices.

In April 1837 some poor labourers in the village of Besthorpe wrote this letter:

> Gentlemen, excuse the liberty we take in troubling you with a second letter, not hearing anything from the first. We now take the liberty of writing to you again upon the subject of emigration to America for we are quite tired of this country and we should be glad to know whether there be any probability of leaving it. For the thought of being ushered into a workhouse with our wives and children and the miseries of starvation and **poverty** makes us quite tired of our native land. For we know that we cannot be worse off than we are. The farmers are using the threshing machines and other machinery so that there are from six to twelve able men that are able to work but cannot get employment.

Think

- What different reasons do the labourers of Besthorpe give for wanting to emigrate to America?

- Who do you think these men might have been writing to?

The historian Gary Howells has studied hundreds of records like these. He says that even very poor people still chose to leave of their own accord. He says that many of these people played a very active part in getting help and money to travel.

A twenty-seven year old labourer called Samuel Simpson left Northamptonshire for South Australia in 1850. As he waited to depart, he wrote this to his clergyman to thank him for his help:

> I am thankful that I leave here on board for another country for I was tired of England Sir.

At the same time, many people chose to **come** to Britain, like Jews from Eastern Europe and over one-and-a-half million Irish people. The Great Irish **Famine** in the mid 1840s forced the Irish to leave in large numbers. By 1851 over a million Irish people had emigrated to the United States of America.

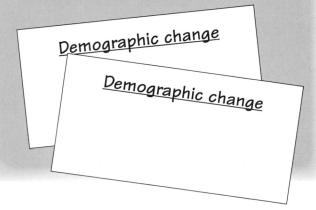

STEP 2

Now make two more Change Cards about demographic change. On your first card describe **where** Europeans went. On your second card explain **why** they emigrated. Write only two sentences on each card. Write in large, bold print (or make your cards using a computer). Put the same little symbol that you designed in STEP 1 on each of your cards.

Demographic change

Demographic change

On the move

The period between 1750 and 1900 also saw new ways of moving people and goods much more quickly. Changes in methods of transport were dramatic compared with what had happened before. These pictures from *The Illustrated London News* sum up the way in which people saw the changes in transport in 1897.

'The Illustrated London News', 1897

Think

What changes does the picture show in:

- transport by sea?
- transport over land?
- quality of roads?

During the period between 1750 and 1900 transport methods improved much, much more rapidly than they had ever done before.

Roads

Better design of coaches, such as narrower wheels, and much better road surfaces, meant that by the 1780s many coaches could go very fast. This table shows you how road and vehicle improvements changed the time it took coaches to travel between London and Manchester.

Year	Journey time
1700	98 hours or more
1760	48 hours
1830	19 hours

From the 1780s coaches were used to carry letters. Before this, letters were carried by postboys on horseback.

Canals

The great expansion of canals began in the 1760s. By the 1790s a national network of canals had been created. Cargo could cross the country from Liverpool to London. The history of canals shows just how fast things were changing. Canals were ideal for transporting heavy goods like coal, but this was not to last. Canals were soon to lose most of their customers ... **to the railway**.

Railways

Railway building was unbelievably fast. In 1832, 166 miles of railway track were open. By 1850 there were 6,559 miles of railway track in use. Railways helped businesses to move raw materials and goods much more quickly than canals ever could. What was more, and unlike the canals, the railways provided good transport for people. See how quickly the railways changed things:

| 1836 | Newcastle to London by road | → 30 hours |
| 1844 | Newcastle to London by rail | → 12 hours |

You needed lots of iron to build a railway, and to build the steam engines that pulled the trains. So the railways gave a huge boost to the iron industry.

You are going to make four Change Cards about improvements in transport. Write only two sentences on each card. Write in large, bold print (or make your cards using a computer). Write one card on roads, one on canals and two on railways.

Design a new little symbol for all four of your cards. Your symbol should show that the cards are about transport.

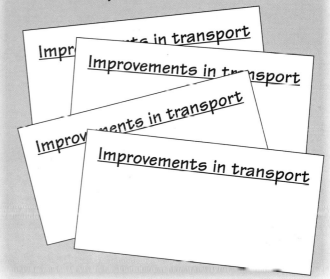

You have now created two sets of Change Cards that give you an overview of two stories of change: **demographic** change and improvements in transport.

However, you do not yet have enough information to explain why some of these changes happened. Transport did not get better just because a lot of clever designers appeared! There were reasons why the people of Britain needed better transport. The more you look at the other stories of change in this period, the more the stories start to connect up.

On this page there are four more stories of change that you can read about in the rest of this book. One of the reasons why change happened so quickly in this period is that all the stories of change are **connected**. When changes happened in one area they affected changes everywhere else.

Changes in industry

New inventions made it possible to spin and weave cloth much more quickly. This meant that the factory owners could make a lot more money.

The factories needed supplies of coal and iron so that the steam engines could work the new machines.

Large buildings, called factories, were needed for the new machines and the many workers who operated them.

Many of the new goods were sold abroad. This is why Britain was called the 'workshop of the world'.

Changes in farming

Wealthier farmers bought strips of land from the poorer villagers. They used these to make larger farms with enclosed fields where they could experiment with new types of crops.

Poorer villagers, who had sold their land to richer farmers, now became landless labourers. Some left the countryside for new jobs in the towns.

The growing populations in the new towns needed food. This helped the farmers to make more money. The food had to be transported to the new towns.

By enclosing their fields, farmers were able to experiment with the selective breeding of animals. These animals could produce more milk or more meat.

Changes in living and working conditions

Conditions in some of the new towns were terrible. Workers lived in tiny houses with no running water and no sewage facilities.

Conditions in the factories were harsh. Young children had to clean machines. Some worked for as long as fourteen hours a day.

Later in the 19th century some politicians passed new laws to improve conditions in the towns. They hoped that this would win them the votes of the working people.

Laws were passed in the 19th century to stop factories from employing very young children and to cut the hours which older children worked.

Changes in government and power

In 1750, only very rich people could vote for a Member of Parliament.

Some of the men who became rich as a result of the **industrial** changes (factory owners and business men) gained the vote in 1832, after a long campaign.

By the early 1800s there were still few Members of Parliament representing the new industrial towns, even though the populations there were growing fast.

In the second half of the 19th century, more and more working men were given the vote.

Thinking your enquiry through

You have made two sets of Change Cards:

- Improvements in transport
- Demographic change

On the page opposite there are another four sets of Change Cards:

- Industrial changes
- Changes in farming
- Changes in living and working conditions
- Changes in government and power

There are lots of different ways of showing how all these changes were connected. You are now going to make three different diagrams so that you can experiment with different ways of connecting everything up.

Diagram 1: Links between the changes

This diagram will link your cards with those on page 12 opposite.

You don't have to draw or write anything for Diagram 1. It is just a warm-up to get you thinking!

Wherever you **think** you can see a **link** between one of your cards and a card on page 12, put your card down, like this:

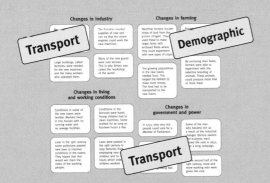

Find as many links as you can. Wherever you think that one of your cards might help to explain one of the changes on page 12, just put your card down!

Diagram 2: Special words to describe the changes

This diagram gives you practice in using special words.

Historians use special words like 'social', 'economic' and 'political' to help them to describe different types of change. This is what these three words mean:

social: things to do with how and where people lived and worked
economic: things to do with money
political: things to do with power

Now try to put all the Change Cards (those you made **and** those on page 12) under one of these three headings. You will need a copy of the cards on page 12. Just arrange all the cards in three columns.

Diagram 3: Overlap diagram for slippery words

This diagram helps you to do some more linking ... and it shows that the special words are rather slippery!

Did you notice that in Diagram 2 there were some cards that fitted into more than one column? Perhaps you need a better diagram – one that will show the overlaps. Words like 'social' and 'political' are rather slippery! Make Diagram 3, like the one below. Try to find a home for all the cards. Remember to use the overlap areas!

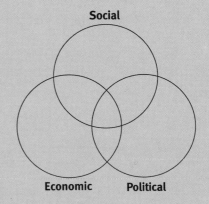

White gold and black misery ②

What lay behind the horrors of the slave trade?

This picture gives you a good idea of how some people relaxed around the year 1750. But behind this scene lay a lot of hard, slow work. The table and chairs would have been hand-made by joiners, the clothes by tailors, the knives and spoons by a cutler and the cups, saucers and plates by a potter.

One of the containers on the table was filled with sugar. The British loved sugar. They used it in tea from China and in coffee from America. They added it to puddings, pies and tarts. Their teeth rotted but their love for sugar grew. Any merchant who could bring raw sugar to Britain was sure to make a great profit. The pure, **refined** sugar became known as 'white gold'.

A portrait painting by Philip Reinagle, eighteenth century

Think

- Why do you think work was slower in 1750 than it is today?

- Why was sugar called 'white gold'?

Your enquiry

As you have seen from the picture above, there is a lot more to some pictures than meets the eye. In this enquiry you will learn just how much hard work and misery went into filling that sugar bowl. You will use three pictures connected to the sugar trade to show just how complicated – and how terrible – the trade in 'white gold' really was.

Down at the docks – Liverpool

A merchant who wanted to bring raw sugar back to Britain needed a ship, a captain and a crew. In 1750, there were no engines on ships, they were powered by the wind. It was a tough life at sea. But despite the dangers and the low pay, men joined trading ships like this one to avoid poverty and unemployment.

Think

● What different materials do you think have been used to make this ship?

A painting of an eighteenth-century trading ship

Between 1700 and 1800 English ports such as London, Bristol and Liverpool grew as trade increased. In 1700, Liverpool was a small, quiet port with a population of around 5,000. By 1800 the population had grown to nearly 80,000. People moved to the city to support the trade which flowed through it. They built ships, made ropes, anchors, and sails, built warehouses, opened inns and shops. Some set up sugar refineries. Merchants who did really well opened banks which helped others to trade at home and overseas.

There were many new jobs at the docks. People had to load and unload **cargo** and keep records of what the ships carried. Some ships traded with Ireland but others went much further. These ships needed supplies of all sorts for their long voyage.

Here are some of the goods they took with them:

For the crew	For trading overseas
Barrels of salted beef	Textiles (cotton cloth from Lancashire)
Candles	Knives and swords (made in Sheffield)
Flour	
Barrels of beer	Guns and gunpowder
Fruit	Beads and glass
Fresh water	Tobacco
Biscuits	Brandy
Iron chains	Iron, copper and brass bars (from Wales or Birmingham)

Think

● What different workers would be pleased that trade from Liverpool was growing?

Sometimes a single rich trader bought all the goods which were to be exchanged. Other ships carried goods paid for by many different people. These people knew that the small amount they **invested** could bring them a fine profit when the ship returned carrying sugar. No wonder the people of Liverpool were excited by the growth of their city. Everyone seemed to be gaining from Liverpool's trade overseas as this source shows:

This great return of wealth, may be said to spread through the whole town. It increases the fortunes of the main adventurers and it contributes to the support of the majority of the inhabitants. Almost every man in Liverpool is a merchant and he who cannot send a bale of cloth will send a box of some other thing. Almost every order of people is interested in a cargo.

From 'The town of Liverpool' by James Wallace, 1795

STEP 1

The picture shows ships being loaded at Liverpool docks in 1750. But it does not show the whole story. Many other people who are not shown in the picture were involved in Liverpool's trade.

Copy out the table below. Use the information in the picture and in the section called 'Down at the docks – Liverpool' to fill in the two columns.

Down at the docks – Liverpool

How people **in** the picture were involved in the sugar trade:	How people **beyond** the picture were involved in the sugar trade:

Capturing the cargo – West Africa

Ships sailed from British ports such as Liverpool to the west coast of Africa. This was **not** the place where they would collect the sugar they wanted. But it was the place where they could unload the goods they were bringing from Britain and exchange them for something even more valuable – black **slaves**.

Since ancient times slaves had been bought and sold in Africa. But when the white Europeans joined in they changed the slave trade dramatically. They wanted to take strong slaves to work in their new lands in America and the West Indies.

The Europeans could not gather all the slaves they needed just by kidnapping Africans from the coast so they made strong trading links with African chiefs. The European traders took goods to Africa which were of great value there. These included fine cloth, metal bars, strong drink, guns and gunpowder. In return, African traders brought men, women and children to be handed over to the Europeans as slaves.

What few Europeans knew – or wanted to know – was that the Africans had built up many remarkable kingdoms over hundreds of years. One of the greatest was the Empire of Songhai, far inland. In 1525, an Arab visitor described the capital city of Timbuktu:

> Here are many shops of craftsmen and merchants. This region yields corn, cattle, milk and butter in great abundance. Salt is brought here from over five hundred miles away. The king has much gold and rides upon a camel. His soldiers ride upon horses. Here are great stores of doctors, judges, priests and other learned men. Books are brought here which are sold for more money than any other goods.

Kingdoms such as Songhai lost their power in the 17th century. In the 18th century, other kingdoms such as Benin became rich through the slave trade.

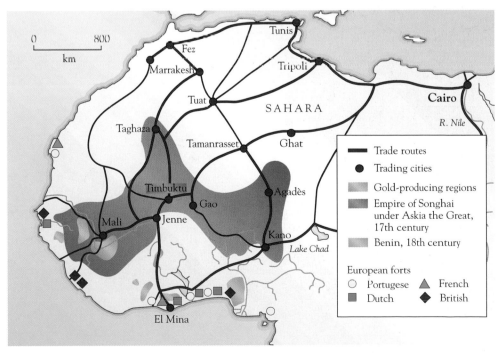

Kingdoms and trade in West Africa, 1500–1800

Map labels: Tunis, Fez, Marrakesh, Tripoli, Tuat, SAHARA, Cairo, R. Nile, Taghaza, Tamanrasset, Ghat, Timbuktu, Agadès, Gao, Jenne, Mali, Kano, Lake Chad, El Mina

0   800
km

Trade routes
Trading cities
Gold-producing regions
Empire of Songhai under Askia the Great, 17th century
Benin, 18th century

European forts
○ Portugese
■ Dutch
▲ French
◆ British

The kings of Benin fought many wars against other tribes. Their soldiers won easily, partly because the kings had bought guns from white slave traders. As they took more land, the kings of Benin encouraged the slave trade. Bands of African raiders from inland tribes attacked villages and kidnapped young men and women. They sold them to other black traders who marched them hundreds of miles to the coast. By 1804, one trader explained that the slave trade:

> … is carried on by a chain of merchants from the coast indefinitely in many directions towards the interior.

Some tribes refused to take part in raids on their neighbours – but these people missed out on the wealth that came from the slave trade and grew weak. In this way power shifted in West Africa. In some areas the population fell alarmingly as parents lost their young, healthy sons and daughters. Kingdoms went to war against each other. Traditional crafts and ways of life were lost.

No one is sure how many slaves were taken from Africa by white traders. Most historians agree that about eleven million Africans were sold into slavery between 1500 and 1850. But even this huge figure doesn't take account of the millions who died as prisoners or who were killed in raids. Sea captains from Liverpool and other ports usually did not know – or care – how the men, women and children had been captured. They just checked the quality of the slaves by looking closely at their teeth and skin, branded the ones they wanted and turned away those who were too old, too young or too weak. The sailors then loaded their ships with their cargo of slaves and with supplies of fresh water, fruit and meat that they bought from African traders.

Think

- Who caused these great changes in West Africa – white traders or African kings?

- Why do you think some crafts and ways of life were lost?

A nineteenth-century print of African slaves being herded to the coast by other Africans

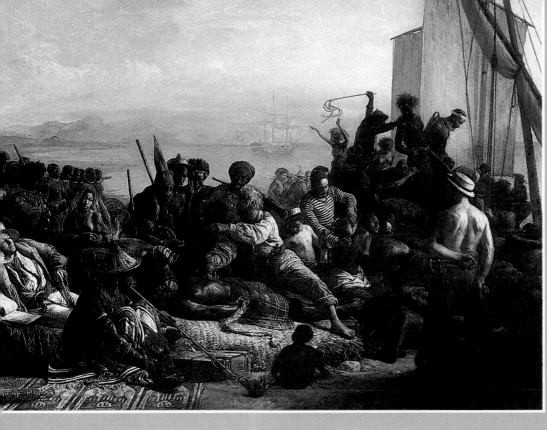

Once again, this picture only shows part of the story of the slave trade in Africa. A lot more lies behind it. Copy the table below. Use the information in the picture and in the section called 'Capturing the cargo – West Africa' to fill in the two columns.

Slave merchants on the coast of Africa
Painted by François-Auguste Baird
in 1832

Capturing the cargo – West Africa

How people **in** the picture were involved in the slave trade:	How people **beyond** the picture were involved in the slave trade:

Going to work – Jamaica

Thousands of slave ships sailed from Africa to North America where the slaves worked growing cotton or tobacco. Many British ships made their way to Jamaica in the West Indies where the slaves grew sugar – white gold.

Some ships were packed with six hundred or more slaves. This plan of a slave ship was drawn in the 18th century. It shows how the Africans were chained together and packed tightly in dark, hot, airless holds below deck. They would be kept there for most of the voyage across the Atlantic Ocean– a journey which could last several weeks. Not surprisingly, many slaves died on the way in these horrific conditions.

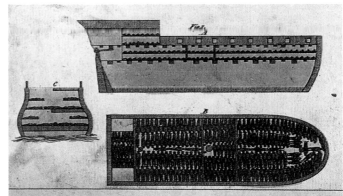

Think

● How many layers of slaves are there?

● If a captain knew that many slaves might die in the crowded holds, do you think he would take more or fewer slaves?

19

Dealers would be waiting at ports in the West Indies or North America to buy the cargo of slaves. If the wind was in the right direction, they could smell a slave ship approaching before they saw it. The dealers usually sold the slaves to **plantation** owners who grew the sugar or cotton that the captain wanted. Growing sugar cane involved back-breaking work in sweltering heat. That was why plantation owners wanted slaves to work in their fields.

Slaves had no rights. They were the property of their master. They could own nothing. They were not allowed to marry but the owners encouraged them to have children who would be new, young slaves for the future.

If slaves committed serious crimes they could have their noses slit, their ears cut off or their faces branded. The most common punishment was whipping. After fighting for freedom in a slave revolt in 1760, one black rebel was burnt alive from his feet upwards. But slaves still revolted – there were over thirty rebellions in the West Indies between 1750 and 1850.

STEP 3

Think

- Why do you think slave ships smelt so much?
- How do you think the plantation owners got the money to buy slaves?

On large plantations the rich, white owner and his family lived in a fine house. The slaves lived in clusters of small huts near the fields. A few worked as servants in the master's house and some were trained as blacksmiths or carpenters. But most worked hard in the fields. Gangs of slaves were controlled by slave drivers.

The slaves
- dug the ground
- spread dung
- weeded the land
- cut the sugar cane
- carried the sugar cane to the mill
- loaded barrels of raw sugar onto ships to be taken to England.

A print showing slaves working on a sugar plantation, 1823

Copy the table below. Use information from the picture and from the section 'Going to work – Jamaica' to fill in the two columns.

Going to work – Jamaica

How people **in** the picture are involved in slavery:	How people **beyond** the picture are involved in slavery:

Journey's end – Liverpool again

Back in Liverpool, the sugar, cotton or tobacco that the slaves had grown was sold at a huge profit. By 1790 Liverpool was making a million pounds each year from the slave trade. But it did not last. In 1787, the **Abolition** Society was formed in Britain to try to end the slave trade. Many of its members were deeply religious Christians. Some were **Methodists** who followed the ideas of their leader, John Wesley. Here is what Wesley wrote in 1774 about the riches of the slave trade:

> It is far better to have no wealth than to gain wealth at the expense of virtue. Honest poverty is better than all the riches bought by the tears and sweat and blood of our fellow creatures.

One **evangelical** Christian, William Wilberforce, worked hard in Parliament to abolish the slave trade. But black people spoke out for themselves as well. Olaudah Equiano was one of several slaves who won their freedom and who wrote books in Britain arguing that the slave trade must end.

In 1807, Parliament banned British ships from trading in slaves. Then in 1833 it set slaves free in all British lands. In 1863, American slaves were also set free. But these 'free' blacks continued to do the hardest work for low pay growing sugar, cotton and tobacco. Meanwhile, many whites continued to look down on them. Laws may change suddenly but it takes longer to change people's attitudes.

Think

- How is our world today still affected by what happened during the years when the slave trade was allowed?

Thinking your enquiry through

Maps like this often appear in school text-books. They show what ships carried as they travelled around the 'slave triangle'. But the map does not show what went on inside each country involved. Write an essay which answers the question, 'What lay behind the horrors of the slave trade?' Write a paragraph on each of the following points:

- how the slave triangle worked (use the map to help you)
- how people in Britain were involved in the slave trade (use the list you made in STEP 1 to help you)
- how people in Africa were involved in the slave trade (use the list you made in STEP 2 to help you)
- how people in the West Indies were involved in the slave trade (use the list you made in STEP 3 to help you)
- a conclusion summing up what you think lay behind the horrors of the slave trade.

Money, mills and machines 3

Why was Quarry Bank Mill so successful?

Look carefully at this illustration of the inside of Quarry Bank Mill. A **mill** is a big factory. This is what the mill might have looked like during its heyday in the 1820s and 1830s.

Before the late 18th century no one had ever seen a factory like this! No one would have believed that such things were possible. No one worked like this. No one even expected to work like this. Quarry Bank Mill is a building that no one could ever have imagined.

Yet in 1784 Samuel Greg built this enormous factory at Styal in Cheshire.

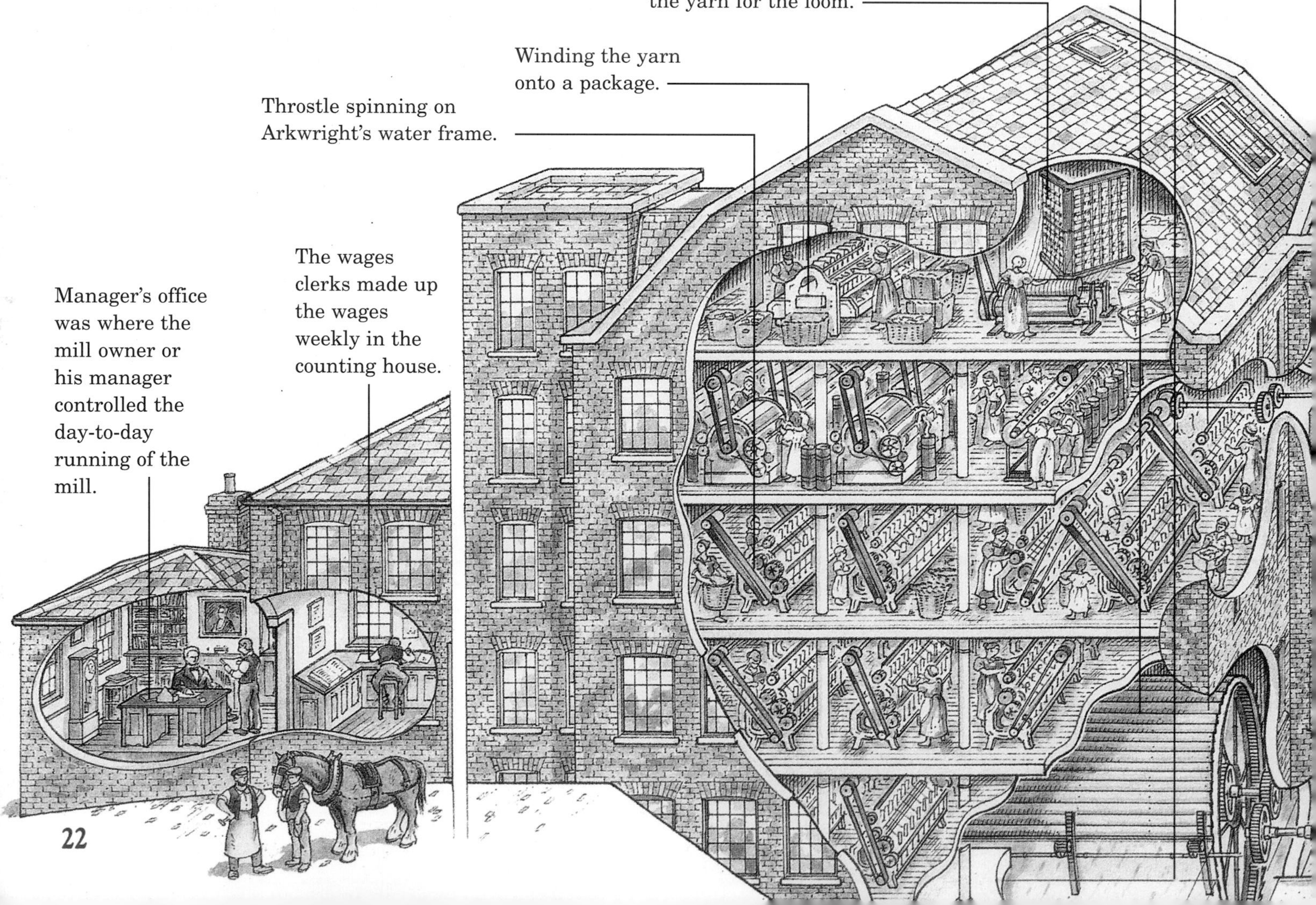
Water from the River Bollin powered the wheel.
The giant water wheel gave power to each floor of the mill.
Warping prepared the yarn for the loom.
Winding the yarn onto a package.
Throstle spinning on Arkwright's water frame.
The wages clerks made up the wages weekly in the counting house.
Manager's office was where the mill owner or his manager controlled the day-to-day running of the mill.

The factory made a lot of money and Samuel Greg carried on improving it. After his death, his sons carried on improving it. They made even more money than he did.

Quarry Bank Mill today

Your enquiry

By the end of this enquiry you will be able to answer the question, 'Why was Quarry Bank Mill so successful?' There are lots of ways of explaining things that happened in the past. But which is the best way?

You are going to look at four ways of answering the question. You will soon see that the success story of Quarry Bank Mill was part of some much bigger stories.

Millwrights had to keep the gears and shafts of the water wheel working.

Carding untangled the cotton.

Reeling wound the cotton into hanks for sale.

Drawing stretched the clean fibres and straightened them.

Mule spinning stretched and twisted yarn to make finer thread. Spinning was a man's job assisted by women piercers who mended any broken threads. In some mills children known as scavengers kept the mule clean of dust and loose thread. They had to crawl under the moving machinery.

Bells marked the arrivals, mealtimes, and departures of the workers.

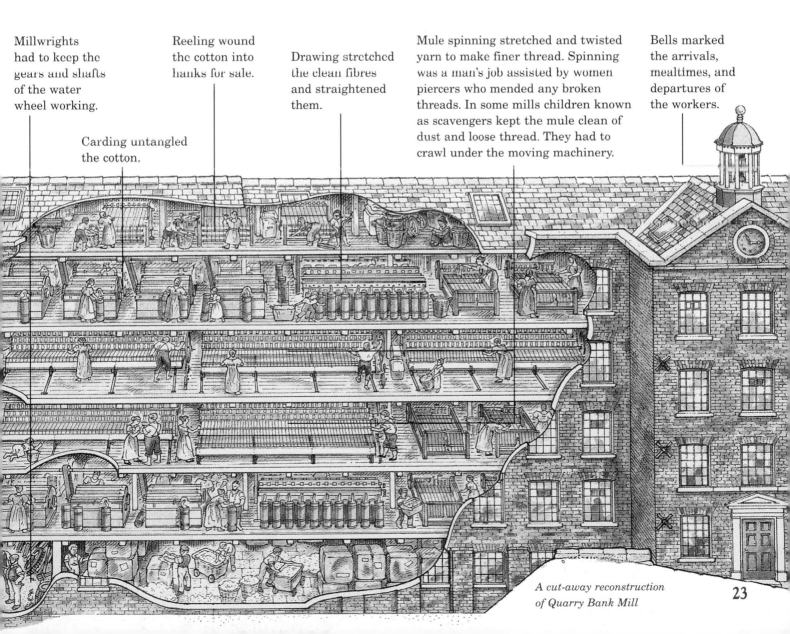

A cut-away reconstruction of Quarry Bank Mill

Explanation 1 – The story of a businessman: Samuel Greg

Samuel Greg came from a very wealthy family of merchants in Belfast. He is marked in red on this family tree.

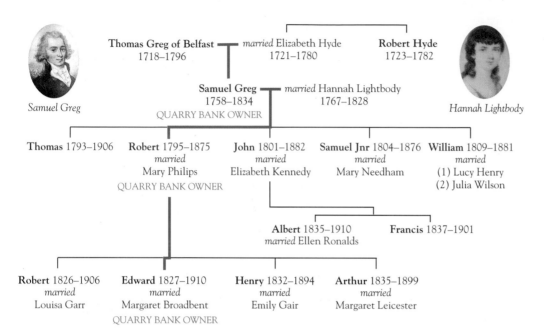

Thomas Greg of Belfast 1718–1796 — *married* Elizabeth Hyde 1721–1780 | **Robert Hyde** 1723–1782

Samuel Greg

Samuel Greg 1758–1834 QUARRY BANK OWNER — *married* Hannah Lightbody 1767–1828

Hannah Lightbody

Thomas 1793–1906 | **Robert** 1795–1875 *married* Mary Philips QUARRY BANK OWNER | **John** 1801–1882 *married* Elizabeth Kennedy | **Samuel Jnr** 1804–1876 *married* Mary Needham | **William** 1809–1881 *married* (1) Lucy Henry (2) Julia Wilson

Albert 1835–1910 *married* Ellen Ronalds | **Francis** 1837–1901

Robert 1826–1906 *married* Louisa Garr | **Edward** 1827–1910 *married* Margaret Broadbent QUARRY BANK OWNER | **Henry** 1832–1894 *married* Emily Gair | **Arthur** 1835–1899 *married* Margaret Leicester

Think

- Find Robert Hyde (Samuel's uncle) on the family tree.

- How old was Samuel Greg when his uncle died in 1782?

- When Samuel Greg died in 1834, who inherited Quarry Bank Mill?

Samuel Greg was adopted by his uncle, Robert Hyde. Robert Hyde lived in Manchester where he already had a successful business as a cloth merchant. Robert Hyde took Samuel into partnership in 1780. On his uncle's death in 1782, Samuel took over the business.

Samuel Greg started to buy property to expand the business. He also decided that he needed to build a very large building in which all his cotton workers could work together. He started to go on long journeys into the countryside around Manchester.

He was looking for a fast-flowing stream. In 1783, he found what he was looking for.

On the River Bollin, at Styal, just north of Wilmslow, he found a place where he could dig a long headrace channel. This meant that there was plenty of water to turn a big wheel very fast. As the wheel turned, it could provide power for all the machines in a mill.

If we dig a long headrace channel, we can make the water fall ten feet onto the wheel!

In 1784, Samuel Greg built the first mill at Styal.

Samuel Greg also built a fine house for his family. Samuel and Hannah were well known among other business people and factory owners from Manchester's new middle classes. They were members of the Manchester Literary and Philosophical Society. They often entertained the visiting speakers to debates at their fine home.

Samuel Greg was also a religious man. Like some other successful business men in Manchester he was not a member of the Church of England. He was a **nonconformist**. He and his wife went to a **Unitarian** church. At the Unitarian church each Sunday, he met many other wealthy business people and their families. Some of these people took a great interest in the education of working people.

In the 1780s many factory workers lived in dreadful conditions. But Samuel Greg was very concerned about the welfare of his workers. He built houses for them on his land. He also built an **apprentice** house for the children who worked in the factory.

Samuel Greg provided education and medical care for the children. But the children still worked very long hours in the mill. Their lives were completely different from the lives of Samuel Greg's children.

In 1830, Samuel's son Robert built a grand mansion at Norcliffe Hall. The house was large and beautiful. It was surrounded by woods and fields. By this time, the Greg family owned other mills too.

The Greg family were now wealthy and powerful.

Norcliffe Hall

Samuel Greg died in 1834. He would have been proud of all his achievements.

STEP 1

Telling the story of Samuel Greg is one way of explaining why there was such a successful mill at Styal. Write a heading:

Explanation 1: The story of Samuel Greg

Under the heading, copy and complete this sentence-starter four times, each time using one of the four different sentence-endings that follow.

Quarry Bank Mill was so successful because …

… Samuel Greg came from a family that was used to finding new ways of making money.

… Samuel Greg was a serious, hard-working, energetic man who was determined to achieve a lot.

… Samuel Greg inherited the family business from his uncle.

… Samuel Greg was clever enough to find a stream where the water could flow fast enough to turn his water wheel.

Now choose one or more code letters to write next to each completed sentence:

M = money   **G** = geography
I = the skill and vision of individuals

Samuel's vision, skill and determination were very important, and so was his choice of place for the mill. But all this information about Samuel Greg still does not **really** explain why the mill was so successful. People were building mills in many parts of Britain. They had not done so before. Now it was happening all over the place! We need to ask **bigger** questions. We need to look for more explanations.

Explanation 2 – The story of the new inventions

Something else was happening. Cloth had been made in Britain for centuries, but the work had always been done in small workshops or in people's cottages. This picture shows an Irish family cotton hand-spinning at home, in the 18th century. The spinning wheels were pushed into a corner when the family wanted to eat.

A great change took place in the last quarter of the 18th century. New inventions were changing the way in which cloth was made.

Machines that could be used at home

Machines that were big and were used in factories

1733
The flying shuttle
Invented by John Kay
Made weaving much quicker

1764
The spinning jenny
Invented by James Hargreaves
Could spin eight yarns at once

1769
The water frame
Invented by Richard Arkwright
Powered by water. Could only be used in factories. Made much stronger thread

1784
The mule
Invented by Samuel Crompton
Made high-quality, strong thread

1786
The power loom
Invented by Edmund Cartwright
Slowly took over all weaving. Powered by water or steam

When Samuel Greg began to build his mill in 1783, he built it to house spinning frames. These spinning frames were large. The workers needed plenty of light so the factory windows were large. The machines needed power from a water wheel. Samuel Greg was using new technology.

Think

Why did Samuel Greg have to pay attention to:

- **where** he built the mill?
- the **size** of the mill?
- the **shape and features of the rooms** in the mill?

Young Robert Greg was always trying to persuade his father to use even newer technology. The newest power looms for weaving could be powered by water or steam.

Samuel was not sure. It was a big risk. When he died in 1834, he had still not agreed to the change. After his death, his son Robert lost no time. In 1836, alterations were made to the building. Quarry Bank Mill soon had power looms, just like Cartwright's power loom. Now they could weave at Quarry Bank Mill too.

Telling the story of new inventions is another way of explaining why there was a successful mill at Quarry Bank. Write a heading:

Explanation 2: The story of new inventions

Copy and complete this sentence-starter three times, each time using one of the three different sentence-endings that follow.

Quarry Bank Mill was so successful because …

… Samuel Greg wanted to use spinning frames as these would spin cotton more quickly and this would make cotton cheaper.

… it was no longer possible to house the new machines in cottages and small workshops.

… it had a strong power source (the fast stream), which is what the new machines needed.

Now write one or more code letters next to each sentence:
T = technological change
M = money   **G** = geography
I = the skill and vision of individuals

Think very hard. Some sentences will need more than one code letter.

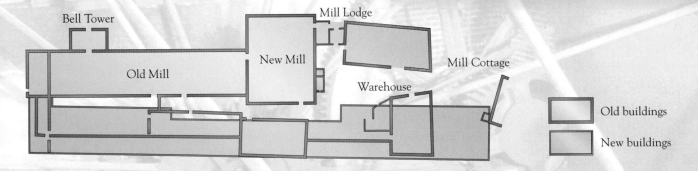

Plan showing when new buildings for weaving were built at Quarry Bank Mill

Explanation 3 – The story of cotton

Something else was happening, too. By the time Robert Greg was putting power looms into his mill at Styal in 1836, cotton had become much more important than wool. Exports of cotton goods were worth only £11,000 a year in the 1740s. This had risen to £17 million by 1820. By 1850, cotton goods were Britain's leading **export**. **But why had cotton become so important?**

Here are four possible reasons.

Reason 2: The supply of raw cotton grew

After North America became independent in 1783 the Americans were free to look for new products to sell. Cotton plantations soon became very successful. In 1793 Eli Whitney invented a 'cotton gin' which helped slaves to prepare cotton 50 times faster than before. Imports of cheap raw cotton from the United States of America into Britain grew.

Reason 3: People spent more money in the 18th century

Some of this money was spent on clothes. There was therefore an increase in demand for cotton.

Reason 1: The population was increasing

The number of people in the British Isles went up from 10.7 million in 1750 to nearly 27.4 million in 1850. **Textile** producers knew they could get rich by producing more. The demand for textiles was growing.

Reason 4: There was a great expansion in trade

Britain was the world's leading trading nation in the late 18th century. British ships carried goods all over the world. By the early 19th century cotton goods made up nearly half of all British exports.

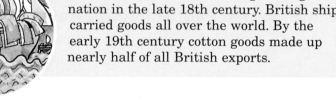

STEP 3

Telling the story of cotton is yet another way of explaining why there was such a successful mill at Styal. Write a heading:

Explanation 3: The story of cotton

Copy and complete this sentence-starter four times, using each of the four different sentence-endings.

Quarry Bank Mill was so successful because ...

... there were more and more people in Britain and they wanted more and more cotton.

... there was more and more cotton available, especially after the Americans started to grow it.

... people in Britain began to spend much more money in the 18th century.

... people abroad were spending more and more money on British goods as Britain expanded her trade all over the world.

Now write one or more code letters next to each sentence:
T = technological change   **M** = money
G = geography **I** = the skill and vision of individuals

Think very hard! You will need to go back and read the four reasons on this page again. Some of your sentences will have more than one code letter!

Explanation 4 – The story of iron, coal and steam

Meanwhile, yet **another** story was taking place! Without it, the first three stories would not have happened. This is the story of cheaper iron and coal. It is also the story of steam power.

Steam engines use coal to heat water and create steam. The pressure of that steam is used to move a piston. In 1766, a Scottish engineer called James Watt made big improvements in the design of steam engines so that they would be more powerful and burn less coal.

In 1781, Watt found a way of getting a steam engine to turn a wheel.

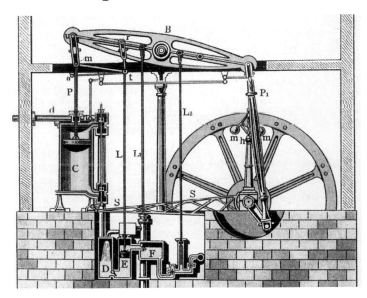

Watt's double-acting condensing steam engine

Think

- What fuel powered this steam engine?
- What materials do you think were necessary to make this steam engine?
- How would steam engines have helped the Greg family?

Steam engines could now be used in factories instead of water wheels.

This steam engine was made possible because of two big developments.

Development 1: New ways of making iron

In 1709, a man called Abraham Darby found a way of making cast-iron using coke. Coke is made from coal. This was a big breakthrough. Iron had always been made from charcoal. By the 18th century, charcoal was becoming scarce and expensive. In 1784, Henry Cort invented a new method of making wrought-iron in a huge coal-fired furnace. So it became cheaper to make iron. Well made iron machinery was essential for the machinery used in the factories.

Big idea: iron makes coal more important!

Development 2: A new role for coal

The new factories depended on coal. It was coal that fuelled the steam engines and the iron foundries.

Big idea: coal makes iron more important!

This diagram helps you to understand the links between iron, coal and steam

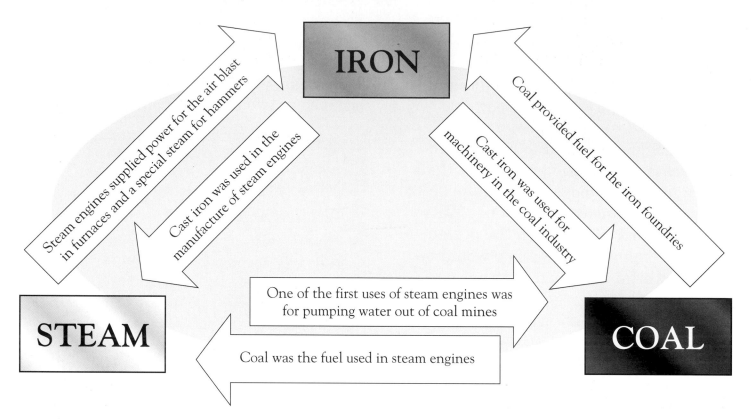

IRON

Steam engines supplied power for the air blast in furnaces and a special steam for hammers

Cast iron was used in the manufacture of steam engines

Coal provided fuel for the iron foundries

Cast iron was used for machinery in the coal industry

One of the first uses of steam engines was for pumping water out of coal mines

Coal was the fuel used in steam engines

STEAM

COAL

Think

- Explain why textile mills needed coal.

- Explain why textile mills needed iron.

- If you had to put another box on the diagram above, called 'Textiles', where would you put it and why?

STEP 4

Write a heading:

Explanation 4: The story of iron, coal and steam

Copy and complete this sentence three times, using the three sentence-endings below:

Quarry Bank Mill was so successful because …

… the use of cheaper coal and better ways of making iron soon made steam engines very profitable.

… new ways of making iron improved machines for spinning and weaving.

… from the 1830s it increased its profits by using weaving looms powered by steam.

Now write one or more code letters next to each sentence:
T = technological change   **M** = money   **G** = geography
I = the skill and vision of individuals

Some sentences may need more than one code letter.

Thinking your enquiry through

You now have two different ways of answering the question, 'Why was Quarry Bank Mill so successful?' You can use the four **big** stories or you can use your new codes or themes.

1 First check your understanding of the four **big** stories. Draw a chart like the one below. Wherever you think there is a strong connection, draw a line from the Quarry Bank Mill story (the **little** story) out to each of the four **big** stories. You will need to go back and read each of the four big stories again first!

2 Now use the **codes** (money, technological change, the skill and vision of individuals, and geography) to build another kind of explanation. Write a big heading: Why was Quarry Bank Mill so successful?

Write one paragraph on each of the four codes. Each paragraph must try to explain why the mill was so successful, using all the facts and ideas that you linked to that code in the STEPs.

You have achieved more than you think!
You have answered a very, very big question:

'Why was there an industrial revolution in Britain?'

1: Big Story The story of the Gregs	2: Big Story The story of the new inventions	Little Story: Quarry Bank Mill	3: Big Story The story of cotton	4: Big Story The story of iron, coal and steam
		1783–84 Samuel Greg built a mill near a fast-flowing stream **1800** Samuel Greg installed a steam engine to provide enough power to run the spinning machines when power was low **1830** By 1822, cotton was selling so well that Samuel Greg built new sheds for packing and sorting. He also built a special new warehouse for all the new raw cotton that was arriving **1836** Robert Greg adapted the mill buildings to house looms for weaving. The mill was now used for spinning **and** weaving **1842** A new 'scutching' building was built. Here the cotton waste was sucked out of the machinery through flues. Iron was used for the equipment and a new iron floor and iron balcony was made as a precaution against fire		

Fingers weary and worn

Why is it so difficult to find out what children's working conditions were really like?

This picture was painted in the middle of the 19th century by an artist called Samuel Bough. It shows some Scottish children and their parents in the fields at harvest time.

Think

- What are each of the people in the picture doing?

- What **message** did the artist want to give people about life in the countryside?

This picture was made in 1867. It shows a gang of children working in the fields.

In the last century, many young children worked in the fields. Other poor children laboured in textile factories or in mines to help with the family income. Gradually new laws, such as the Mines **Act** of 1842 and the Factory Acts of 1833 and 1847 changed all this. Today, we would be shocked at the idea of children as young as nine working for twelve hours a day in a mill or a mine or field – it would be against the law!

It was not easy to change the laws about how children should work. Some people felt strongly that the children's working conditions were too harsh and cruel but others disagreed. Sometimes these two groups **exaggerated** the facts to fit their own point of view. The writing and pictures which they produced were often **biased**. This means that their accounts give a **one-sided** view of what children's working conditions were like.

Think

- What is happening in the picture?
- What **message** did the artist want to give people about life in the countryside?

Think

- In what ways might these two pictures show biased views of children's work in agriculture?

Your enquiry

In this enquiry you will use lots of different sources to find out about children's working conditions in mills and mines. Many of these sources give us a **biased** view. They may provide **unreliable evidence** about children's working conditions. At the end of the enquiry you will understand why it is so difficult for historians to find out what children's working conditions were really like.

Children in the mills

The development of factories was one of the most important changes that took place between 1750 and 1900. Factory owners needed a supply of cheap labour. Children were ideal. They were paid low wages. Sometimes mill owners could get orphan children from workhouses. These children worked for nothing other than food and clothing. Work in the factories was very tiring for young children. The machines did not stop and needed constant attention. The **overseers** made sure the children worked as hard as possible.

Working conditions for factory children caused much argument in the 19th century.

- **Some people**, known as factory **reformers**, thought that children were treated in a brutal way. They wanted to introduce new laws to protect factory children.

- **Other people**, including many mill owners, wanted things to stay as they were.

The sources produced by factory **reformers** and the sources produced by some mill owners give us very different messages about children's work in factories.

Background to Source 1

This picture was printed in a book called *The History of Cotton Manufacture in Great Britain*. The book was published in 1835 and was written by Edward Baines. Baines was editor of a newspaper called *The Northern Mercury*. The newspaper was widely read by northern mill owners. Edward Baines often supported the mill owners' point of view.

Source 1

Think

- In what ways does the picture suggest that the mill was a pleasant place to work?

- Why do you think Edward Baines would want a pleasant picture of a mill for his book?

Background to Source 2

In 1831, the government set up an enquiry into children's working conditions in factories. Hundreds of children were asked about their hours of work, wages, accidents, health and beatings. The commissioners then produced a written report. There are three main reasons why this source might be biased:

1 It is possible that factory reformers might have told some of the children what to say in order to make conditions seem particularly bad.

2 The commissioners might have asked 'leading questions' which they knew would get a certain kind of answer.

3 The commissioners might have picked out the worst examples to include in their report.

For these reasons historians must use the report very carefully. However, the evidence from the government enquiry does give us detailed and first-hand evidence of factory conditions. Even if some of the details are misleading or inaccurate it can still tell us about the types of problems which children faced.

This extract is taken from the *Report of the Select Committee of Factory Children's Labour, 1831–32*. It is part of an interview with Charles Burns, a fourteen-year-old worker in a Leeds textile mill:

Source 2

At what age did you begin work in the mills?
I was nearly eight years old.
What were your hours of working?
From half past five in the morning till eight at night.
How often were you allowed to make water [go to the toilet]?
Three times a day.
Could you hold your water [urine] all that time?
No. We were forced to let it go.
Did you spoil and wet your clothes constantly?
Every noon and every night.
Did you ever hear of that hurting anybody?
Yes, there was a boy died.
Did he go home ill with attempting to suppress his urine?
Yes, and after he had been home a bit, he died.
Were you beaten at your work?
If we looked off our work or spoke to one another we were beaten.
What time of day was it you were most beaten?
In the morning.
And when you were sleepy?
Yes.
Was the mill very dusty?
Yes.
What effect did it produce?
When we went home at night and went to bed we spit up blood.
Had you a cough with inhaling the dust?
Yes, I had a cough and spit blood.

Think

● Why are sources like this one particularly useful for finding out about children's working conditions?

● Find two examples of leading questions in this interview.

● In what ways might this source give us a biased view of working conditions in the factories?

Source 3

Background to Source 3

This picture of children working in a textile mill appeared in a novel written by Frances Trollope in 1840 called *The Life and Adventures of Michael Armstrong, Factory Boy*. It was about an orphan boy who started work in a factory at the age of six and who was treated terribly. Frances Trollope based her book on the story of a real factory apprentice called Robert Blincoe.

Think

● What is happening in the picture?

● How do you think the picture might present a biased view of children's working conditions?

STEP 1

Choose one of the sources in this section.

1 Explain in what ways it provides **unreliable** evidence about children's working conditions in textile factories.

2 Explain in what ways it provides **reliable** evidence about the factories and how children worked in them.

You will need to think carefully about:

● **the background of the source.** Who produced the source and why? How did they get their information?

● **the content of the source.** Does it seem as if the author or artist is trying to get across a strong message?

Children in the mines

In the 19th century many children faced the dangers of work in coal mines. As the demand for coal increased, more and more children were employed in the mines. Men and older boys worked as 'hewers', cutting the coal with picks. Women and younger children hauled the coal along dark tunnels to the shaft bottom where it was loaded into baskets and winched to the surface. Children as young as eight worked as 'trappers', opening the doors to let the coal trucks pass along the tunnels.

The following sources can tell us a lot about work in the mines, but it is not always easy to find out what children's working conditions were **really** like.

Background to Source 1

These extracts are from the parish register of Radstock in Somerset. The burial register is particularly useful because it recorded the cause of death and the age of the people concerned:

Think

- What **do** these extracts tell us about children's work in coal mines?
- Why is this source likely to give us reliable information about children's deaths in the mines?
- What **don't** these extracts tell us about children's work in coal mines?

Source 1

30 August 1820
Frederick William Bond age twelve
Head fractured by kick from a horse
in Clandown coal pit

14 December 1821
William Bourne age nine
Killed by falling down Ludlow coal pit
24 fathoms (122 feet)

26 November 1824
George Chappel age eight
Killed by falling down Ludlow coal pit

4 October 1835
John Ashman age eleven
Killed by falling down the Tyning coal pit

16 November 1842
Joseph Parfitt age nine
Killed by bad air in a coal pit

Background to Source 2

In 1840, the government set up a royal **commission** to investigate working conditions in the mines. Over the next two years the four commissioners and twenty sub-commissioners interviewed hundreds of men, women and children from coal pits all over the country. The final report of the commission filled three volumes when it was published in 1842. It gives us very detailed evidence about children's work. However, some people at the time opposed reform of the mines. These people claimed that the report **exaggerated** bad conditions. They said that the commissioners asked leading questions and that some children lied about their work. They also claimed that the pictures showed the very worst cases of child labour in the mines.

Source 2

Janet Cumming,
a coal bearer, eleven years old

I go down with the women at five in the morning and come up at five at night. I carry the large bits of coal from the wall face to the pit bottom. It is some weight to carry. The roof is very low. I have to bend my back and legs and the water comes frequently up to the calves of my legs. Have no liking for the work. Father makes me like it. Never got hurt, but obliged to scramble out of the pit when the bad air was in.

Alexander Gray,
a pump boy, ten years old

I pump out the water in the under bottom of the pit to keep the men's rooms [coal face] dry. I am obliged to pump fast or the water would cover me. I had to run away a few weeks ago as the water came up so fast that I could not pump at all. The water frequently covers my legs. I have been two years at the pump. I am paid 10d. a day. No holiday but the sabbath. I go down at three, sometimes five in the morning, and come up at six or seven at night.

Think

- Why is the *Report on the Employment of Children in Mines* such a useful source for historians?

- Think of two problems which historians face when using the text and pictures from this source.

Background to Source 3

Many mine owners were worried by the *Report on the Employment of Children in Mines*. If the government decided to stop children working in mines, the mine owners' profits would fall.

The Marquess of Londonderry owned many pits in the north-east of England. In 1842, he attacked the report in the House of Lords. This is an extract from his speech:

Source 3

The commissioners expected and desired to find ill-treatment of children. Their instructions were to examine the children themselves, artful boys and ignorant young girls, and to put questions in a manner which suggested the answer.

The trapper is generally cheerful and contented, and to be found occupied with some childish amusement, such as cutting sticks, making models, and drawing figures with chalk on his door.

Think

- Why did the Marquess of Londonderry attack the report?
- What did the Marquess of Londonderry think about the commissioners?

Choose one of the sources in this section.

1 Explain in what ways it provides **unreliable** evidence about children's working conditions in coal mines.

2 Explain in what ways it provides **reliable** evidence about the mines and how children worked in them.

Thinking your enquiry through

You have seen that historical sources do not always provide historians with reliable evidence about children's working conditions in the 19th century.

Use as many sources from this enquiry as you can to explain why it is so difficult to find out what children's working conditions were really like.

You may want to use some of these sentence-starters in your answer:

Finding out about children's working conditions is difficult because …

Some sources suggest that …

However, other sources suggest that …

One problem with the sources is …

Another problem with the sources is …

The biggest problem facing historians is …

'A perfect wilderness of foulness'

5

Why were the cities so unhealthy?

This picture shows Leeds in 1885.

By 1885, Leeds was one of the biggest **industrial** cities in Britain.
During the first half of the 19th century thousands of people flooded
into the city to look for work. They found jobs in factories
and workshops making cloth, leather and machines.
They also found dirt, disease and early death.

Think

- What buildings can you see?

- Use the picture to help you think of two good words to describe Leeds in 1846.

40

The main industrial cities in Britain

Your enquiry

In this enquiry you will discover what it was like to live in Leeds and other industrial cities shown on this map. You will find out about people's poor housing, their toilets (or lack of them!) and the awful diseases which threatened their lives. By the end of this enquiry you will be able to **describe** what the cities were like and **explain** why they were so unhealthy.

A visitor to Leeds in 1848 described the city as 'a perfect wilderness of foulness'. For many people, Leeds was a grim place. Poor labourers were crowded together in muddy streets and yards. Their houses had no running water. They often shared a **privy** with many other families. Few of the streets had sewers. Killer diseases like tuberculosis, typhus and cholera were common. The average age of death for a Leeds labourer in the 1840s was nineteen.

Housing and health

In the early 19th century more and more people moved to towns and cities to find work. Houses were needed – and fast. The factory workers had to live as close as possible to their place of work. There were no cars, buses or bicycles and people started work at six o'clock in the morning. The houses of the labouring poor were therefore crowded together in narrow, terraced streets around the smoky factories.

Some of these houses were well built, but many were not. The builders often wanted to make a quick profit. The houses they put up were small, cheap and soon became very nasty. In the first part of the 19th century there were no rules to make sure that houses were properly built. Many builders took advantage of this. Some of the worst houses were built in terraces which were joined to the row behind. We call these houses back-to-backs.

In the 1850s Edward Hall, a missionary who helped the poor people of Leeds, described what it was like to live in one of these houses:

> They are built back-to-back with no possibility of good ventilation. The cellars are used for storing coal and food. In the coal department there are often kept hens, rabbits and pigeons. The families do all their cooking, washing and other work in a room ten feet by fourteen feet. There is another room this size for sleeping.

From the Annual Report of the Domestic Mission Society, Leeds, 1858

Think

- Why do you think back-to-back houses were unhealthy places to live?

In the middle of towns land was very expensive and builders squeezed in as many houses as they could. Many poorer houses in Leeds and other cities were built in around **yards**. These were entered by a narrow alley from the street. The yards were cheap places to live, but they were dark, dirty and very unhealthy.

A photograph of a Leeds yard

By far the most unhealthy localities of Leeds are close squares of houses, or yards, as they are called. Some of these are airless from the enclosed structure. They are unprovided with any form of underdrainage or convenience or arrangements for cleansing and are one mass of damp and filth. The ashes, garbage and filth of all kinds are thrown from the doors and windows of the houses upon the surface of the streets.

From a Report on Sanitary Conditions in Leeds by James Smith, 1845

A cellar dwelling

Think

- Why do you think the yards were often 'airless'?

- Why were the yards so dirty?

Think

- Describe the features of this cellar which made it such an unhealthy place to live?

Some of the very poorest people in Leeds could not even afford to rent a back-to-back house in a yard. Instead, they crowded below ground in the **cellars** of other people's houses. Robert Baker, a surgeon and factory inspector from Leeds, described the cellar dwellings which he visited in the 1830s:

I have been in one of these damp cellars without any drainage. Every drop of wet and every bit of dirt have to be carried up into the street. There are two beds covered in sacks for five people. There is hardly anything to sit on but a stool and a few bricks. The floor is wet in many places and a pig is kept in the corner.

STEP 1

Think carefully about the information you have looked at in the section called 'Housing and health'. Use the information to begin a list of reasons why cities in the 19th century were so unhealthy. Divide your list into two columns like the ones below. Your first column should **describe** what people's houses were like. Your second column should **explain** the reasons for poor housing.

What people's houses were like	Reasons why housing was poor
Many houses were built back-to-back.	New houses had to be built very quickly because so many people came into the towns.

43

Water and waste

Today we take clean water for granted. Our local councils make sure that new houses have piped water, drains and sewers. For most of the 19th century this did not happen. It took many years for councils to accept that it was their job to make sure that everyone had clean water and proper sewers. Builders did not think it was their job either. They just wanted to put up houses quickly.

Very few people had clean water piped to their houses.

- Some people queued for water at stand-pipes in the street and carried it home in buckets, pans and kettles.
- Some bought clean water from water-sellers.
- Some collected rainwater in barrels.
- Some carried it in buckets from the river.

What they did not know was that dirty water could kill them.

People collecting water in London.
A line drawing from the Illustrated Times, 1867

Most streets in Leeds were built without drains to take away the waste water. The poorer houses were built on boggy land by the river where it was difficult to lay pipes. Sometimes builders made deep holes in the ground, but these were soon blocked. In the poorer districts, pools of stinking water filled the yards and alleys. This is what Robert Baker wrote when he visited the house of a poor Leeds man and his family in 1842:

> He has very bad health and his wife has rheumatism. The water in front of the house has collected from various sources. The yard has never been dry since he came to it. There is a sump-hole, a great depth in one corner, made by the landlord, to take away the water, but it is full of deposit. The stench is often so bad, and especially after rain, that he and his wife cannot bear it.

Think

- What method are these people using to obtain their water?

The terrible smells came not only from waste water, but also from the **privies** which poor families shared. This is how one observer described the Leeds privies in 1845:

> The privies are few in proportion to the number of inhabitants. They are open to view in front and rear and are inevitably in a filthy condition. They often remain without any removal of the filth for six months.

The privies were not connected to sewers. Instead, the sewage collected in cesspits under the ground. From time to time night-soilmen cleaned out the cesspits. They piled the sewage in dunghills and sold it to local farmers. But some land-lords did not like to pay night-soilmen and cesspits were left to overflow. This picture shows what could happen.

Think

- What has happened to the cesspit in this picture?
- Why was this cesspit a danger to people's health?
- Why do you think the cesspit was allowed to overflow?

A cross-section of a Leeds yard

STEP 2

Use the information in the section called 'Water and waste' to add to the list of reasons why the cities were so unhealthy that you began in STEP 1. Divide your list into two columns like the ones below. Remember that your first column should **describe** what the water supply and sewerage were like and your second column should **explain** why they were so bad.

What water supply and sewerage were like	Reasons why there was poor water supply and sewerage

Dirt and disease

Blue Bell Fold was a small cul-de-sac of twenty houses in one of the poorer parts of Leeds. The houses were built next to a stinking stream which flowed into the River Aire. On 26 May 1832, a two-year-old child who lived in one of the houses suddenly began to vomit and have diarrhoea. Within a few hours the child's body had turned a blue-black colour. The eyes sank into the head. The skin went cold. Family and neighbours watched in horror as the child struggled for breath and died.

The child from Blue Bell Fold was the first recorded person in Leeds to die during the terrifying cholera epidemic which hit the city in the summer of 1832. Within a few months, over seven hundred people had died of the disease.

In 1831 and 1832, Britain's first cholera epidemic killed 31,000 people. The disease returned again in 1848, 1853 and 1866. Cholera was just one of the killer diseases which people feared in the 19th century. Other diseases such as tuberculosis, typhoid, typhus, scarlet fever and measles killed tens of thousands of people in the 1830s and 1840s.

Today we can prevent these diseases, but in the first part of the 19th century people did not have our medical knowledge. They knew that there was a connection between dirt and disease, but no one had shown that germs were the cause of disease. Many doctors believed that the sewers and dirty streets gave off a poisonous gas, called 'miasma', which caused illness.

Even when doctors showed a connection between dirty drinking water and cholera, many councils were slow to take any action. Providing the labouring poor with clean water and sewers would have cost money. Many middle-class rate-payers in Leeds and in other cities did not want to see their money spent on such schemes.

Use the information from the section called 'Dirt and disease' to finish the list of reasons you began in STEPs 1 and 2. Arrange your ideas under these two headings:

How people were affected by disease	Reasons why disease was so common

Thinking your enquiry through

So why were towns and cities in the 19th century so unhealthy? You are now going to write an essay to answer this question.

Organise your essay in five paragraphs:

- Introduction
- Housing and health
- Water and waste
- Dirt and disease
- Conclusion

In each of the three middle paragraphs make sure you **describe** what conditions were like and **explain** the reasons for these conditions.

Remember that historians always have to **support** what they say with facts. You will need to look back at the different sections in this enquiry to find details which support your ideas.

You may want to use some short quotations from the written sources to make your ideas stronger.

Pauper palaces

6

Why did people disagree about the New Poor Law?

This overgrown, disused building was once a workhouse. It was built in Thurgarton, a village in Nottinghamshire. For many years labouring people in Thurgarton and the surrounding villages lived in fear of this building. Even today there are elderly people who want to forget the workhouse. Some people say that the building should be pulled down.

Think

- Think of three good words to describe the building in this picture.

Hundreds of **workhouses** like the one at Thurgarton were built all over the country in the years after 1834. They were part of a new system set up to deal with the poor. The New Poor Law forced many people who were old, sick or unemployed to enter a workhouse if they wanted help. Life in the workhouse was miserable. Families were split up. **Paupers** were forced to work long hours. There was little food and punishments were often harsh. Many people thought that the workhouses were worse than prisons.

Not everyone hated the workhouses. Many middle-class people who paid rates to look after the poor thought that the New Poor Law was needed. These people believed that if conditions in the workhouses were harsh, labourers would be more likely to work hard in their jobs. Many rate-payers thought that the unemployed would only find work if they were afraid of the workhouse.

The New Poor Law is a good thing. It has cut the cost of poor relief and has made the poor work harder.

The workhouses are like prisons. They are cruel places. It is unfair to treat the poor in this way.

A supporter   **A critic**

Your enquiry

This enquiry is about people's different attitudes towards the new workhouses that were built after 1834. The New Poor Law caused huge disagreements. It had many supporters, but also many critics. In this enquiry you will be either a critic or a supporter living at that time. If you are a critic, you will collect information to explain what was wrong with the New Poor Law. If you are a supporter, you will collect information to show that the New Poor Law was a success. At the end of the enquiry you will write a letter to *The Times* newspaper to explain your views.

The New Poor Law

Since Elizabethan times, poor people were looked after in the parishes where they lived. Overseers of the poor in each parish collected the Poor Rate from people who owned land and houses. This money was then used to help sick, old and unemployed people. In some parishes, poorhouses were built where paupers worked in return for food and clothes. However, most parishes could not afford to build poorhouses. Instead, overseers gave money to paupers who were allowed to stay in their own homes. This was known as **outdoor relief**.

From 1750 this system of poor relief came under great pressure.

- The growing population and spread of enclosures meant that more and more people had no work.

- Food prices were rising. Wages were lagging behind. Some parishes even started giving outdoor relief to people with jobs because some poor labourers earnt so little.

- The cost of outdoor relief went up and up. Rate-payers were forced to pay more and more.

By the 1830s the old system of poor relief was at breaking point. New threshing machines on the farms were forcing labourers out of work and wages dropped still further. When some parishes tried to reduce Poor Law payments, there were riots. **The government knew that something had to be done to deal with the problem of poverty.**

In 1834, a New Poor Law was passed. It introduced three new ideas.

1 The parishes were grouped together in Poor Law Unions. The Board of Guardians for each union now looked after the poor in each union.

2 From 1834 the rules said that anyone who needed outdoor relief had to enter a workhouse.

3 Conditions inside the workhouse had to be worse than conditions for the lowest-paid labourer outside.

STEP 1

Use the information in this section to begin collecting ideas for your letter. Remember that you are living at that time.

Critic
List as many reasons as you can to explain why you are against the New Poor Law.

Supporter
List as many reasons as you can to explain why you support the New Poor Law.

Regulations

The people in charge of the New Poor Law were called the Poor Law Commissioners. After 1834 the Poor Law Commissioners produced plans and regulations to help the Poor Law Unions set up new workhouses. This plan shows the kind of workhouse which the Poor Law Commissioners suggested for 200 paupers.

Think

- How does the plan show that families were split up when they entered the workhouse?

- How does the plan show that paupers were meant to be treated properly in the workhouse?

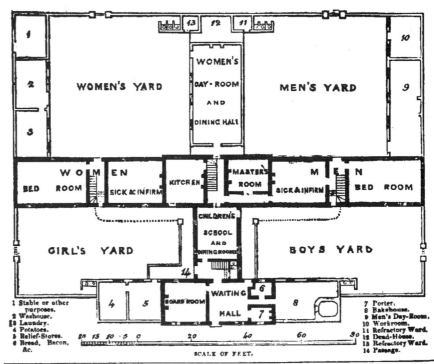

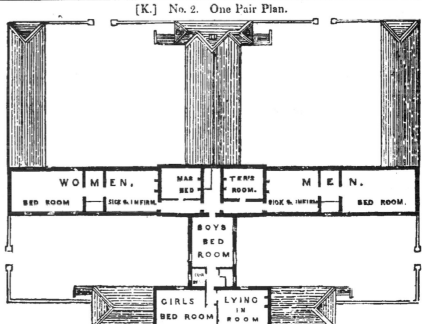

[K.] No. 2. One Pair Plan.

Plan of a workhouse from the commissioners' report, 1834

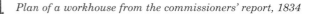

In 1847, the Poor Law Commissioners issued a very detailed set of workhouse regulations. These four rules are taken from the regulations. They tell us how paupers were meant to be treated when they first entered the workhouse:

1 As soon as the pauper is admitted he shall be placed in a receiving room where he shall be examined by the Medical Officer.

2 If the Medical Officer finds any disease of mind or body, the pauper shall be placed in the sick ward or in such other ward as the Medical Officer shall direct.

3 If the Medical Officer finds the pauper to be healthy, the pauper shall be placed in the part of the workhouse according to his class.

4 The pauper shall be thoroughly cleansed and shall be clothed in workhouse dress. His own clothes shall be cleansed and returned to him when he leaves the workhouse.

Think

● How do these regulations show that the Poor Law Commissioners wanted paupers to be treated properly in the workhouse?

The new workhouses were not meant to be cruel places, but the Poor Law Commissioners wanted them to be strict. The regulations included clear rules about behaviour.

A pauper who was found doing any of these things was to be **given only bread and potatoes for two days**:

- Making a noise during silence
- Using bad language
- Threatening to hit another pauper
- Not keeping clean
- Pretending to be sick
- Entering part of the workhouse which was for another class
- Refusing to work
- Playing cards
- Climbing over the workhouse wall
- Misbehaving during church services
- Returning late after an outside visit
- Disobeying an officer of the workhouse

A pauper who did any of these things was to be **locked up for a day**:

- Insulting the Master or Matron
- Disobeying the Master or Matron
- Hitting another pauper
- Damaging workhouse property
- Getting drunk
- Causing a disturbance during prayers

STEP 2

Use the information in the section called 'Regulations' to collect more ideas for your letter.

Critic
Give three reasons why you think the new workhouses are too harsh.

Supporter
Give three ways in which the new workhouses are meant to treat people properly and encourage good behaviour.

Reality: Gressenhall Workhouse

The rules and regulations laid down by the Poor Law Commissioners only tell us what the new workhouses were **supposed** to be like. To get a better idea of what life was **really** like in a workhouse we need to use records from the workhouses themselves. Very few paupers wrote about their experiences, but the Board of Guardians often left detailed information. These extracts are all taken from the records left by the Board of Guardians of Gressenhall Workhouse in Norfolk:

Daily routine

Regulations to be Observed in the Workhouse
Hour of Rising   5.45am
Interval for Breakfast   6.30–7.00am
Time for Work   7.00–12.00 noon
Interval for Dinner   12.00–1.00pm
Time for Work   1.00–6.00pm
Interval for Supper   6.00–7.00pm
Time for going to Bed   8.00pm

These times to be notified by ringing a bell and during the time of meals silence to be maintained.

Regulations in Gressenhall Workhouse, 1851

Punishment

John Craske and Anne his wife were brought before the Board for stealing bread. They shall be put in the dungeon for 24 hours and their diet shall be bread and water for the remainder of the week.

From the 'Minute book of the Board of Guardians', 1841

Food

		BREAKFAST		DINNER						SUPPER	
		Bread.	Gruel.	Suet Pudding with Vegetables.	Bread.	Cheese.	Butter.	Meat Pudding with Vegetables.	Broth.	Bread.	Cheese.
		oz.	Pints.	oz.	oz.	oz.	oz.	oz.	Pints.	oz.	oz.
SUNDAY.	Men	7	1½	-	-	-	-	14	-	7	1
	Women	6	1½	-	-	-	-	12	-	6	¾
MONDAY.	Men	7	1½	-	7	-	-	-	1½	7	1
	Women	6	1½	-	6	-	-	-	1	6	¾
TUESDAY.	Men	7	1½	-	7	1	-	-	-	7	1
	Women	6	1½	-	6	-	¾	-	-	6	¾
WEDNESDAY.	Men	7	1½	-	7	1	-	-	-	7	1
	Women	6	1½	-	6	-	¾	-	-	6	¾
THURSDAY.	Men	7	1½	14	-	-	-	-	-	7	1
	Women	6	1½	12	-	-	-	-	-	6	¾
FRIDAY.	Men	7	1½	-	7	1	-	-	-	7	1
	Women	6	1½	-	6	-	¾	-	-	6	¾
SATURDAY.	Men	7	1½	-	7	1	-	-	-	7	1
	Women	6	1½	-	6	¾	-	-	-	6	¾

DIETARY FOR ABLE BODIED PAUPERS OF BOTH SEXES.

OLD PEOPLE of 60 years of age and upwards, may be allowed 1 oz. of Tea, 4 oz. of Butter, and 4 oz. of Sugar per Week, for those whose age and infirmities it may be deemed requisite.

CHILDREN under 9 years of age, to be dieted at discretion ; above 9 to be allowed the same quantities as Women.

SICK to be dieted as directed by the Medical Officer.

Dietary for able-bodied paupers of both sexes, 1836

Complaint

A complaint has been made to the Guardians of the use of bad language by Thomas Butcher, the porter, towards the pauper inmates of the workhouse. It appears that the complaint is well founded. Thomas Butcher to be reprimanded for his conduct with a view to his immediate dismissal in the event of any repetition of such offence.

From the 'Minute book of the Board of Guardians', 1859

The Master and Mistress

The Board of Guardians give their thanks to Mr and Mrs Pinson for their services as Master and Matron of Gressenhall Workhouse for nearly seven years. They have shown kindness to the inmates and have reduced the expenditure below that of any other Union. They have prepared more than one hundred orphan children to be useful members of society. The Board also give their thanks to Miss Pinson for her duties as schoolmistress to the Gressenhall Workhouse.

From the 'Minute book of the Board of Guardians', 1844

The schools

I have this day inspected the schools. The boys answered remarkably well in the Scriptures. Indeed, their religious knowledge would do credit to any school. Their arithmetic is fair and they possess greater knowledge of geography than is usually the case in schools of this description. Their reading is still much below their other attainments and their writing might be improved. I must say that it is impossible for one man to attend properly to a school of 80 boys.

Extract from a school inspector's report on the schools at Gressenhall Workhouse, 1849

Leaving the workhouse

Artists	1	Printers	1
Army	8	Shoemakers	5
Carpenters	2	Tailors	4
Gentlemen's service	11	Schoolmasters	4
		Farm service	12
Harnessmaker	1	Other	
Not known	12	employments	26

Destinations of boys who left Gressenhall Workhouse, 1845–53

STEP 3

Use the information in the section called 'Reality' to collect more ideas for your letter.

Critic
Give three ways in which life was harsh in the new workhouses. Find examples from the Gressenhall Workhouse to back up each of your ideas.

Supporter
Give three ways in which the workhouses treated people properly and encouraged good behaviour. Find examples from the Gressenhall Workhouse to back up your ideas.

Reactions

As more and more workhouses were built across the country people became divided in their views. These are the kinds of things which people said at the time:

> The new workhouses have improved the morals of the poor. The public houses and beer shops are much quieter and there is not as much drunkenness.

> The workhouse is held in great dread.

> The poor would rather die than go into a workhouse.

> Parents and children are dying in the workhouse without seeing each other.

> The Poor Rates have been greatly reduced and the old and sick are still cared for.

> The New Poor Law has saved huge sums of public money.

> People who could not be made to work have now become good labourers.

> People are more willing to look for work than they were before 1834.

> The separation of man and wife is not what our good Lord intended.

> The New Poor Law treats poverty as a crime.

> The New Poor Law is cruel. It should be called the starvation law.

> Freedom, food and clothing are the birthright of every Englishman.

> In the north of England the New Poor Law is causing great distress. The mill workers are rioting and many workhouses have yet to be built.

Decide which of these statements were made by critics and which were made by supporters.

Add these to the ideas for your letter.

Thinking your enquiry through

It is 1854. You live in Norfolk, close to Gressenhall Workhouse. You feel very strongly about the way in which the opening of the new workhouses has affected the lives of the poor. You have decided to write a letter to *The Times* newspaper. Use the information you have collected in STEPs 1 to 4 to write a letter explaining your views. You may want to use the sentence-starters below to begin your paragraphs.

Sir,
Over the last twenty years the New Poor Law has been the source of much debate and disagreement on the pages of your newspaper. I write as a supporter/critic of the New Poor Law, believing that …
(Use some of the ideas in STEP 4.)

The New Poor Law …
(Use the ideas you collected in STEP 1.)

The regulations governing the new workhouses are …
(Use the ideas you collected in STEP 2.)

Life for the paupers in my nearest workhouse at Gressenhall is …
(Use the ideas you collected in STEP 3.)

Riot and reform 7

When was Britain closest to revolution between 1815 and 1832?

In 1789, there was a violent revolution in France. The people took over the government, and the king, queen and thousands of nobles lost their heads under the heavy blade of a new and deadly machine – the guillotine. To rich and powerful people, the guillotine became a symbol of all that they hated about revolutions: it stood for death, blood and chaos.

The guillotine

By 1815 the revolution in France was over. But there was still the possibility of other revolutions in other countries. This cartoon appeared in England in 1819. On the left is a fierce monster which looks strangely like a guillotine! The men on the right are the rulers of Britain.

Think

- How has the cartoonist made the monster look frightening?

- What are the British rulers doing and saying?

'A Radical Reformer' by George Cruikshank, 1819

56

Your enquiry

The cartoon shows us that some people in 1819 were really afraid that there might be a British revolution – but in fact it never happened. Although Britain went through a very unsettled time between 1815 and 1832, the government never completely lost control. In this enquiry you will find out why so many people disliked and challenged the government at this time and you will make a display to show how close you think Britain came to having a revolution.

It is hard to know how close a country is to having a revolution. This historian has studied many different revolutions. She has come up with a useful checklist to help you.

A country may be **quite close** to a revolution if **some** of these things are happening:

- The working **classes** are poor and have no power
- The middle classes are rich but have no power
- The rulers and upper classes are rich and refuse to share power
- The middle classes and working classes join forces
- The government starts to make changes but then stops
- The poor are even more hungry than usual
- The army disobeys the rulers

A country is **very close** to revolution if **all** these things are happening at the same time!

Keep turning back to this list as you read about the events in Britain between 1815 and 1832. Use it in each STEP to help you to decide how close Britain was to a revolution at different times.

The underlying problems

There were several reasons why Britain was so unsettled between 1815 and 1832. Here are some of them:

Problem 1 – New ways of working

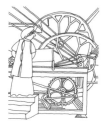

In the new industrial towns, men, women and children worked long hours in bad conditions for low wages. These workers wanted change – but the government did nothing to help them.

Problem 2 – New wealth

Factory owners and other traders were getting richer. They were confident and proud – but they felt that the government was ignoring them.

Problem 3 – New ideas

The French Revolution helped to spread new ideas. Some writers dared to say that people should have equal rights.

Problem 4 – An old system of government

By the start of the nineteenth century, Britain had been ruled in more or less the same way for hundreds of years. Some people wanted to see changes or reforms to the system of government. These people were called **radicals** and they made complaints like these:

This country is run by a **rich king** and **rich lords** and **rich Members of Parliament**. No one votes to choose the king. No one votes to choose the Lords and **only rich men are allowed to vote** for MPs!

It's been the same for **hundreds of years.**

It's not fair!

What about the middle class of people? **What about** the poor? **What about** the women? Don't they matter at all? Can't they have a vote?

We need **big changes** and we need them now! But I'm not sure about letting women vote.

Think

- Which of the underlying problems on this page match up with the historian's checklist on page 57?

1 Begin to make your display. Copy the outline below onto a large sheet.

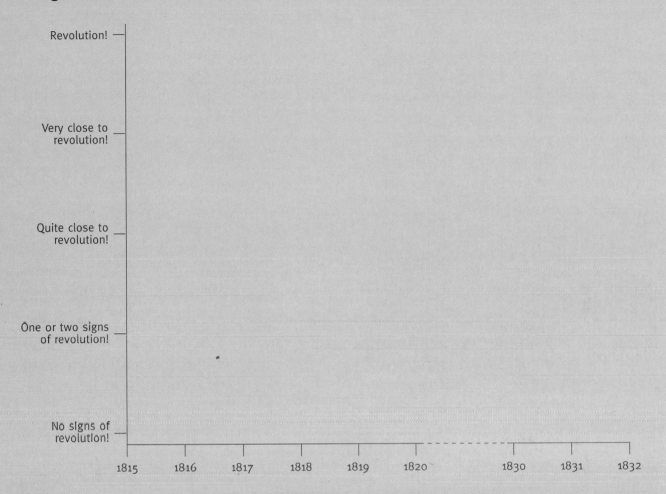

2 Make four Information Cards to stick in the area underneath the graph. Each card must sum up one of the underlying problems which lasted all through the period from 1815 to 1832. Use the section called 'The underlying problems' to help you. Here is an example:

Underlying Problem 1

Factory workers were poor and worked hard. They were angry that the government did not help them.

Years of violence – 1816 to 1817

The Spa Fields Riot – 1816

A war with France started in 1793. It lasted almost non-stop until 1815 when the French leader, Napoleon, was beaten at the Battle of Waterloo. During this war, traders in Britain had been making ships, guns, ammunition and uniforms. But now these were not needed and trade slumped:

- businesses closed down
- many workers lost their jobs
- wages were very low
- bread prices were very high.

All over the country radicals planned demonstrations to demand reforms. They felt that the government would have to treat everyone more fairly if the poor had the right to vote. The government at that time was run by the Tory Party. Tories did not want any changes in the voting system. They **absolutely refused to pass any reform.**

In December 1816, radical leaders in London organised a meeting to be held in Spa Fields, just outside the city. Many middle-class radicals did not attend. They thought some of the organisers were too extreme.

At the meeting the crowds got out of control. A mob broke into a gunsmith's shop. They armed themselves and marched off towards the city. Some were carrying the French revolution-ary flag. Before they got very far they were stopped by the Lord Mayor and some soldiers. Three hundred people from the crowd were arrested and the riot was broken up.

The Derbyshire Rising – 1817

In 1817, taxes and bread prices were still high and there was still a lot of unemployment. There were riots all around Britain. The government sent spies to discover what the radicals were planning now.

Cartoon of the crowds at Spa Fields by G. Cruikshank, 1816

One of the spies had the code name, Oliver. He travelled around the north of England and won the confidence of many radical groups. He told them that masses of people were all set to revolt in every district and encouraged them to join in. He then told the government in London that a revolution was being planned.

In Derbyshire, some poor, unemployed textile workers believed Oliver. Under their leader, Jeremiah Brandreth, they armed themselves with pikes and guns and set out to capture Nottingham. Oliver had told them that thousands more would join them – but no one did. A troop of soldiers from Nottingham marched out to stop the rebels. The rebels dropped their weapons and fled.

Brandreth and three other leaders were executed. This sad attempt at a revolution was over – but we will never know if Brandreth and his friends would have acted without Oliver's encouragement.

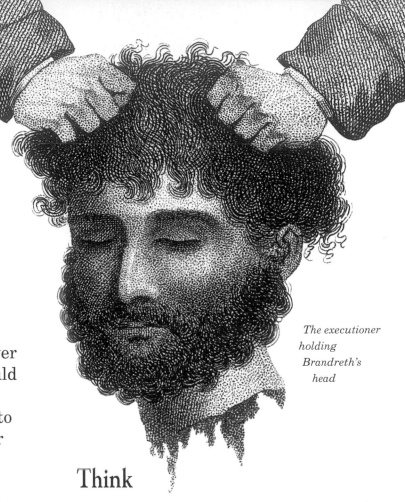

The executioner holding Brandreth's head

Think

- Do you think the Derbyshire Rising was a real attempt at revolution?

- Do you think the government was right to use spies like Oliver?

STEP 2

Look back at the section called 'Years of violence – 1816 to 1817'.

1 Make two Information Cards. Make one about the Spa Fields Riot and the other about the Derbyshire Rising. Make very short notes about what happened, when it happened and why.

2 Now look at the checklist on page 57. Use it to decide if Britain in the years 1816 to 1817 was very close to revolution, very far from revolution or somewhere in between. Use the scale on the left of your display outline to decide where each Information Card belongs on your display. Glue each card in the right place.

Years of violence – 1819 to 1820

The Peterloo Massacre – 1819

In 1819, unemployment and poverty were still serious problems. On 16 August, there was a meeting of more than 60,000 people in St Peter's Fields, Manchester. Henry Hunt, a famous radical, spoke to the crowds. Most were unemployed or poor workers. They were peaceful although some carried banners saying 'Reform or Death'.

As Henry Hunt was speaking, the magistrates ordered some soldiers to arrest him. One of the crowd, a weaver called Samuel Bamford, later claimed that:

> … the troops waved their sabres over their heads and then, striking spurs into their horses, dashed forwards and began cutting the people. Their sabres were wielded to cut a way through naked held-up hands and defenceless heads. Then chopped hands and wound-gaping skulls were seen. Women, maids and tender youths were sabred or trampled.

From 'The life of a radical' by Samuel Bamford, 1844

In ten minutes 400 people were wounded and eleven were killed, including two women and a child. Hunt was arrested and imprisoned.

People were deeply shocked. Some called this event the Peterloo Massacre. The name mocked the 'brave' soldiers who rode into the crowds at St Peter's Fields as if they were beating the French at the Battle of Waterloo in 1815.

One cartoonist drew the scene, clearly showing that he was on the side of the crowds.

Think

- Do the sources on this page show that the crowds wanted a revolution?

'Britons strike home' by George Cruikshank, 1819

The Cato Street Conspiracy – 1820

'The Cato Street Conspirators' by George Cruikshank. 1820

Hunger, unemployment and high taxes continued into 1820. It was too much for some extreme radicals. In January, a small group met in secret at Cato Street, London. They planned a daring conspiracy (plot).

Their leader was a working-class radical called Arthur Thistlewood. One of the men – called Edwards – encouraged Thistlewood to blow up all the leading government ministers. Thistlewood agreed. He and his friends were working alone, but they believed they could take over the whole country.

On 23 February 1820, a band of government agents burst into the house. They arrested all the plotters – except Edwards. Edwards was a government spy. He had led Thistlewood and the others **into a trap**.

Thistlewood stabbed and killed one of the agents attempting to arrest him. He and the other leaders were executed. Thistlewood was the last person in England to have his head cut off – but only after he had been hanged!

Think

- Thistlewood had only a small group. Does this mean he had no chance of starting a revolution?

STEP 3

Follow all the instructions given in STEP 2 – but this time make your Information Cards about the Peterloo Massacre and the Cato Street Conspiracy. Remember to use the checklist on page 57.

Years of violence – 1831 to 1832

The Reform Riots of 1831–32

Between 1820 and 1830 conditions improved. The government faced far less violence. It made a few reforms which pleased the radicals – but it **still** did not change the voting system.

In 1830, a new king, William IV, came to the throne. Soon afterwards there was a general election. The **Whig** Party formed the new government. They had promised to reform the voting system and most voters now seemed to think this was a good idea.

MPs in the House of Commons put forward their ideas for a Reform Act – but the House of Lords rejected it. Most lords were strong Tories and they refused to pass reforms no matter what MPs or voters wanted.

People who cannot vote

Voters

MPs

The Lords

An engraving showing troops breaking up a Reform Riot in Bristol in 1831

The rich landowners in the House of Lords were blocking reform – and Lords could not be replaced by an election. People's anger turned into violence – especially as there was another time of bad harvests and hunger in 1831. There were serious riots all over Britain. In Nottingham the castle was burnt down and in Bristol a mob burnt the bishop's palace.

Think

- Why would voters be so angry when the Lords blocked the plans for reform?

In December 1831, the Whigs tried **again** to get a Reform Act through Parliament. Once **again** the Lords blocked it. The Whigs' leader asked William IV to make 50 new Whig lords who would vote for the Reform Act. The king refused.

Think

● Why might this cause a revolution?

All around Britain people were furious. In Birmingham a middle-class banker called Thomas Attwood suggested that everyone stop paying taxes. Attwood began to organise a massive march to London by 200,000 people from the middle and working classes. There were rumours that Attwood's supporters were persuading soldiers in Birmingham to join their side.

William IV and the lords were scared. In the end they could see that the Reform Act had to be passed. They agreed to let the Reform Act through. It became law in May 1832 and ever since it has been known as the **Great Reform Act**.

Most radicals did not think the 1832 Reform Act was **great** at all. It gave the vote to most middle-class men but it ignored the working classes completely. The radicals were left wondering what to do next.

* Read the next enquiry to see what they tried.

STEP 4

Follow all the instructions given in STEP 2 – but this time make one Information Card about the Reform Riots of 1831–32. Remember to use the checklist on page 57.

Thinking your enquiry through

1 Write down the year and event when you think Britain was closest to a revolution.

2 Use the historian's checklist on page 57 to explain why you chose that event.

The Chartist challenge

What did different people think about Chartism?

This letter was written by William Corah to his father on 18 August 1842:

> Dear father
>
> "Spread the Charter through the land.
> Let Britons bold and brave join in hand."
>
> I write you these lines from the point of death.
> I must now inform you of the state of our town.
> We have had meetings every night this week.
> They assembled at night to the tune of 20,000
> men or upwards and swore that by the ghost of
> many a murdered Englishman and Englishwoman,
> they would not stop until the People's Charter
> becomes the Charter of the land.

Think

- Which of these words and phrases best describes the mood of William Corah:
  - very determined
  - couldn't care less
  - angry
  - excited
- What does the writer of the letter want to happen?

William Corah lived in Leicester. He was a **Chartist**. The Chartists wanted change. They put their demands in a **charter**.

In Leicester many Chartists worked in the textiles industry. They were finding it harder and harder to get work. Men like William Corah hoped that Parliament would accept the demands in the Charter. They believed that this would make their lives better.

A *very useful source*

William Corah was clearly on the side of the Chartists. His letter suggests that he was full of energy, determination, hope and bravery. He seems to be desperate for the Chartists to succeed. We could say that he was **biased** in favour of the Chartists. It is possible, therefore, that he was exaggerating Chartist activities in the town. It is possible that he was going 'over-the-top' in his descriptions.

However, we can still learn a great deal from the letter. It tells us about the hopes and fears of William Corah. This type of source can tell us about the **beliefs, attitudes and views** of some Chartists in 1842.

Your enquiry

In this enquiry you will examine many different types of source. They are all about Chartism and they are all biased. You are going to work out **what each of these sources is useful for.** At the end of the enquiry you will imagine that you are a researcher working for an historian who is trying to answer the question 'What did different people think about Chartism?' You will produce a report on some of the sources. But to do this, you must first learn a little more about the Chartists ...

The story

In June 1832, the Reform Act was finally passed. It had been a long struggle. Working-class and middle-class people had joined together in that struggle. Now many working people felt betrayed. They were bitterly disappointed. The 1832 Reform Act did not give the vote to working people. Working people still had no power. **So their struggle for the right to vote went on**.

In 1836, a group of London working men drew up a charter. This People's Charter demanded six important political reforms. Those who supported these demands were called Chartists. The Chartists wanted a new, fair system of voting. They wanted all men over 21 to have the vote. They also wanted all MPs to be paid. At that time working people could not become MPs.

This is the text of a Chartist handbill.

The Chartists presented huge petitions to Parliament *three times*. Each time, Parliament rejected the petition.

 ## *The first petition – 1839*

By May 1839, over one-and-a-quarter million people had signed the demand that Parliament grant the People's Charter. The petition was taken to London. Parliament rejected it by a vote of 235 to 46. This led to violence. There was a rising in Newport in South Wales. 22 Chartists were killed.

 ## *The second petition – 1842*

In 1842, there was a lot of unemployment. Poverty and hunger were widespread in industrial areas. This led to a lot of support for the Chartists. This time, over three-and-a-quarter million people signed the petition. It took 50 people to carry the petition to London.

The Six Points
OF THE
PEOPLE'S
CHARTER.

1. A VOTE for every man twenty-one years of age, of sound mind, and not undergoing punishment for crime.

2. THE BALLOT.— To protect the elector in the exercise of his vote.

3. NO PROPERTY QUALIFICATION for Members of Parliament—thus enabling the constituencies to return the man of their choice, be he rich or poor.

4. PAYMENT OF MEMBERS, thus enabling an honest tradesman, working man, or other person, to serve a constituency, when taken from his business to attend to the interests of the country.

5. EQUAL CONSTITUENCIES, securing the same amount of representation for the same number of electors, instead of allowing small constituencies to swamp the votes of large ones.

6. ANNUAL PARLIAMENTS, thus presenting the most effectual check to bribery and intimidation, since though a constituency might be bought once in seven years (even with the ballot), no purse could buy a constituency (under a system of universal suffrage) in each ensuing twelvemonth; and since members, when elected for a year only, would not be able to defy and betray their constituents as now.

The procession taking the Chartist petition to Parliament in 1842

Once again, Parliament rejected the petition, this time by 287 votes to 49. Once again, this was followed by violence. There were strikes and riots. Some strikers took the plugs out of the boilers of the steam engines so that all work in the factories stopped. These strikes became known as the Plug Plots.

Think

- Why do you think that so many people signed the petition in 1842?

- Why do you think that many strikers attacked the factories?

- William Corah wrote his letter (page 66) in 1842. Can you work out from his letter whether or not he supported violence?

 ## The third petition – 1848

1848 saw the final Chartist petition. This time the Chartists had high hopes. They planned to meet on Kennington Common in London. They hoped that 500,000 people would come. The plan was to march to Parliament.

The government was worried. The Duke of Wellington prepared troops and police. Nearly 200,000 Special Constables were enrolled, but only 20,000 Chartists came. The disappointed crowd left quietly.

Parliament rejected the People's Charter for the third and last time by 222 votes to 17. There were a few small riots in London, **but Chartism was never the same again**.

Different types of Chartist

It is not very surprising that the Chartists failed. No government of the time would ever have accepted their ideas. However, there is another important reason why the Chartists failed. They were divided amongst themselves. They had different views about how to achieve their aims.

There were two main groups of Chartists, the Moral Force Chartists and the Physical Force Chartists.

Physical Force Chartists were prepared to use force to persuade the government to change things.

Moral Force Chartists wanted to change things through writing, speaking, better education and peaceful persuasion.

The **Physical Force Chartists** were led by a fiery, powerful speaker called Feargus O'Connor. He had a huge following.

William Lovett was the leader of the **Moral Force Chartists**. He was disgusted by the violence of the Plug Plots in 1842.

Working people sometimes chose Moral Force Chartism or Physical Force Chartism according to the different kinds of problems that they faced. This is an extract from an account by a man who travelled in the Burnley area of Lancashire in 1842. The handloom weavers in Lancashire were very angry because the new factory machines were taking away their work.

Groups of idlers stood in the street, their faces haggard with famine, and their eyes rolling with a fierce and uneasy expression. I found them all Chartists, but with a difference: the handloom weavers linked to their Chartism a hatred of machinery, which was far from being shared by the factory workers. The factory workers disapproved of the use of physical force, while the handloom weavers strongly urged an appeal to arms. I heard some call openly for the burning down of mills.

From 'Tour of Lancashire' by Cooke Taylor, 1842

Think

- What does the writer of the source tell us about the views of handloom weavers?

- What does the writer of the source tell us about the views of factory workers?

- Why do you think that so many handloom weavers became Physical Force Chartists?

Source challenge 1

Chartists encouraged each other by singing songs. These songs were a way of building up their courage and of spreading the Chartist message. Each of the sources on this page is a verse from a different, popular Chartist song. Each shows how strongly the Chartists felt. They also show that not all Chartists had the same beliefs!

This verse was written by someone who wanted to encourage others to kill. It was used as evidence against four men accused of plotting a rebellion in the summer of 1839.

In tyrant's blood baptize your sons
And every villain slaughter.
By pike and sword your freedom try to gain
Or make one bloody Moscow of old
    England's plain.

Think

- Find all the words in this verse which suggest **violence**.

- Would this verse have been sung by a Moral Force Chartist or by a Physical Force Chartist?

This is a verse from a very different Chartist song that was popular in 1842:

Cannon balls may aid the truth
But thought's a weapon stronger
We'll win a battle by its aid –
Wait a little longer.

Think

- The verse that begins with 'Cannon balls' looks as though it might support violence too. But it does not! Try to explain what the verse means.

- Would it have been sung by a Moral Force Chartist or a Physical Force Chartist?

The next verse is from another Chartist song. The 'lion of freedom' is Feargus O'Connor. Many Chartists adored O'Connor. His rousing speeches inspired his followers. When he died in 1855 about 50,000 people followed his hearse.

The lion of freedom comes from his den,
We'll rally around him again and again,
We'll crown him with laurels our
    champion to be,
O'Connor, the patriot of sweet liberty.

STEP 1

What do these sources tell you about:

- what different types of Chartists thought, felt and believed?
- why some people criticised, mistrusted or feared the Chartists?
- how some people came to learn about Chartist activities and the Chartist message?

Source challenge 2

This cartoon appeared in *Punch* in 1848. It is not trying to show a real Chartist procession. It is poking fun at the Chartists because many of the signatures on the third Chartist petition were forged. Some Chartists even forged the signatures of Queen Victoria and the Duke of Wellington! 'Pugnose' and 'Longnose' were two of the made-up signatures.

Cartoon from 'Punch', 1848

Think

- List all the ways in which the cartoon makes fun of the Chartists.

- Why would this cartoon have been very damaging for the Chartists?

STEP 2

What can this source tell you about:

- why some people criticised, mistrusted or feared the Chartists?

- how some people came to learn about Chartist activities?

Source challenge 3

The next two written sources tell us about William Cuffay, a Chartist leader. He was born in 1788 on a ship coming to England from the West Indies. His father was a black slave born on the island of St Kitts. His grandfather had been taken there from Africa.

When William grew up he became a tailor. Like many London tailors he became more and more involved in politics. In 1840, he was chosen by the Westminster Chartists to be a delegate to the Chartists Metropolitan Delegate Council.

Picture of William Cuffay (1788–1870)

William was a Physical Force Chartist. In 1848, he was put on trial for plotting to set fire to buildings in London. He was sentenced to be **transported** to Tasmania. For the rest of his life he worked for political rights for the Tasmanian people.

This is part of the speech that William Cuffay made in court before the sentence of transportation was passed.

Think

- What do you think William Cuffay meant when he said he had been 'taunted by the press'?

- Which parts of this source suggest Cuffay's courage and determination?

- Why do you think that there was so much prejudice against Cuffay?

My Lords, you ought not to sentence me. This has not been a fair trial. My request to have a jury of my equals was not granted. The next reason that I ought not to be sentenced is the great **prejudice** that has been raised against me. Everybody that hears me is convinced that almost all of the newspapers of this country, and even other countries, have been raising a prejudice against me. I have been taunted by the press, and it has smothered me with ridicule. It has done everything in its power to crush me.

I crave no pity. I ask no mercy. As I have been an important character in the Chartist movement, I laid myself out for something of this sort from the start. But a great many men of good moral character are now suffering in prison only for arguing the good cause of the Charter. However, I do not despair of its being carried out.

William Cuffay complained that the newspapers were against him. However, it is important to remember that some newspapers supported the Chartists. This newspaper article was written about William Cuffay just after he was transported in 1849:

> He was loved by his own order who knew him and appreciated his virtues. He was ridiculed and denounced by a press that knew him not and had no sympathy with his class. He was banished by a government that feared him. For as long as honesty and honour are admired, so long will the name of William Cuffay, a son of Africa's oppressed race, be remembered.

From 'Reynolds Political Register', a Chartist newspaper published by George Reynolds, a Chartist from Derby

Think

- What do you think 'loved by his own order' means?

- Who do you think this newspaper article was written *for*?

- How might William Cuffay's own family background have inspired him to struggle for the Chartists?

STEP 3

What can these two sources tell you about:

- what different types of Chartists thought, felt and believed?

- how some people came to learn about the Chartist message and Chartist activities?

- why some people criticised, mistrusted or feared the Chartists?

Source challenge 4

Our last source was written by a woman from the upper classes. She was Lady Palmerston, wife of the Foreign Secretary. Here, in her diary, she gives her account of what happened in 1848:

> The Admiralty and all the offices were garrisoned and provisioned as if for a siege, cannon placed on the bridges and the Duke of Wellington's arrangements beautifully made. There was great alarm in all quarters, uncertainty of what number might come in from the manufacturing districts, and the very great number of foreigners in the country. Two hundred thousand Special Constables were sworn in, and, all higgeldy piggeldy, peers and commons, servants, workmen, and all kinds of people. It was thought the people from Kennington Common were going to force their way into the Houses of Parliament and there were frightful reports of these people being armed with guns and pikes and pistols and daggers and knives. But when the Chartists found their own numbers so very short of what they expected, and no sympathy from the middle classes, or soldiers, they gave up all hopes of revolution.

Think

- How do you think that reports of Chartist activities sometimes became exaggerated or inaccurate?

- Pick out all the words or phrases from Lady Palmerston's account which showed that she was frightened of the Chartists.

What can this source tell you about:

- what different types of Chartists thought, felt and believed?

- why some people criticised, mistrusted or feared the Chartists?

Thinking your enquiry through

You are a researcher. You are going to write two source guides for an historian. Remember that this historian is trying to answer the question, 'What did different people think about Chartism?' Choose two contrasting sources. Make a source guide for each source. Make your source guides quick and easy to understand. Make detailed notes on each source under these headings:

Where does the source fit into the Chartist story?

Go back to the section called 'The story' (pages 68 to 70) and make notes on all the background relevant to this source.

What will the historian need to be careful about?

You need to make a note of these things:

- **when?** (When was the source written?)

- **who?** (Do we know what kind of person wrote it? What guesses can we make about the background of the person or people who wrote it?)

- **why?** (Why was it written? What was its purpose? Who was it written for?)

These things might make a source unreliable for **some** facts and details.

How might the source be useful for your historian?

This will be your longest section! List all the ways in which the source might be useful for answering the big question, 'What did different people think about Chartism?' Use the answers you gave in the STEPs.

'Dizzy'
Was Disraeli a failure?

The Ladies' Gallery, House of Commons
From 'The Illustrated London News', 1870

These ladies have come to this special gallery overlooking the House of Commons. Although the notice says 'Silence is requested', some of the ladies are chatting. Others are staring out of the grill. Perhaps they have come to see Mr Benjamin Disraeli – one of the great debaters in Parliament, the leader of the **Conservative** Party and a great favourite with the ladies of London.

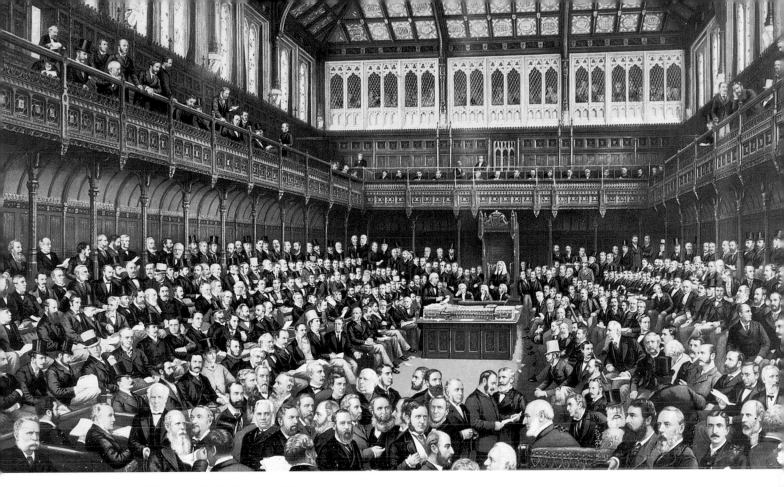

Painting of the House of Commons by F. Sargent, 1882

Think

- Find the Ladies' Gallery in this painting.

- Why do you think that there was a special gallery just for women?

This painting shows you what the House of Commons looked like when it was full.

When Disraeli died in 1881, the nation mourned. The queen had adored him and had recently made him Earl of Beaconsfield. His Conservative supporters, particularly the ladies, wore yellow primroses in memory of him. He was remembered as a great Prime Minister and national leader,

but was he?

Photograph of Disraeli

Your enquiry

In this enquiry you will decide whether you think that Disraeli deserved to be remembered as a great Prime Minister. You will look at his record as a leader and compare what he said with what he did.

A party formed from all classes?

Benjamin Disraeli was Prime Minister of Britain in 1868 and then again between 1874 and 1880. He came from a Jewish family, but joined the Church of England. He made flowery speeches and many of his fellow MPs thought him rather odd. When he first appeared in Parliament he wore green velvet trousers, a canary-yellow waistcoat, shoes with yellow buckles and his hair in ringlets.

However, once he became Prime Minister people soon learnt to take Disraeli seriously. He re-organised the **Conservative** (or **Tory**) Party. He tried to make it popular with the people. It was not enough for the Conservatives just to fight changes. They had been doing this for years. If the Conservatives were to beat Gladstone, the powerful **Liberal** (**Whig**) leader, they would have to have ideas of their own.

Disraeli wanted the Conservative Party to appeal to many more people. He believed that the Conservatives would be stronger if they were supported by people from all social classes. He wanted the party to have support from the working classes and the middle classes as well as from the rich and powerful. He told the Conservatives:

Benjamin Disraeli as a young man, by Daniel Maclise

> Gentlemen, the Tory Party, unless it is a national party, is nothing. It is a party formed from all classes, from the highest to the most homely.

Think

- What do you think Disraeli meant by 'the highest to the most homely'?

- Why do you think that Disraeli wanted to change the Conservative Party?

But did Disraeli achieve his aim? And did he **really want** to include the working classes in the first place? You must judge whether what he did matched what he said. This is what happened …

Back in 1866, when the Liberal government tried to pass a Reform **Bill** giving the vote to many working-class men, Disraeli and the Conservatives opposed the bill. They claimed it was dangerous to give the vote to men with no education. In 1866, the Conservatives became the government and Disraeli was an important minister. The demand for reform was still strong and popular. An angry crowd clashed with police in London and tore down the railings of Hyde Park.

An engraving of a Reform League protest at Marble Arch

It was clear that reform was needed to calm things down. Disraeli took a great risk. Even though he had stopped the Liberal bill the year before, he now led the way in getting a Conservative bill passed in 1867. This became the **1867 Reform Act**.

Better-off working-class men in towns and cities were given the vote. There were 638,000 of them. This raised the number of men who could vote to over two million.

Disraeli called this Reform Act a 'leap in the dark'. He meant he was not sure whether the new voters would support the Conservatives or not. He hoped many would vote for his party out of gratitude.

He was proved wrong.

The Liberals accused Disraeli of double standards. They claimed that he had stolen their idea. In 1868, Disraeli lost the general election to Gladstone and the Liberals. So Disraeli did not get the support from the workers that he had hoped for.

It was not until 1884 that working-class men in the countryside got the vote.

STEP 1

Write a heading:
Disraeli's record (1)

Underneath it copy this sentence:
Disraeli said that the Conservative Party 'is a party formed from all classes'.

Now you must judge whether he achieved this or not. Draw two columns like this:

Success	Failure

Choose facts and ideas from pages 78–79 to go into each column.

Looking after the people?

Between 1874 and 1880 Disraeli passed lots of laws. Disraeli claimed that these laws would gain his party 'the lasting affection of the working classes'. Here is part of a speech in which he promised to help the working classes. The other boxes tell you about some of the laws he passed.

Another great aim of the Tory Party is the improvement of the people. Pure air, pure water, and the inspection of unhealthy houses ... the first consideration of a Minister should be the health of the people.

1875 Artisan's Dwelling Act

This gave local councils the right to rebuild slums. However, the councils did not *have* to rebuild them and few councils did so as it was too expensive. Only in Birmingham were large areas of the city rebuilt. This law did little to change the lives of ordinary people.

1875 Acts concerning Trade Unions

The Liberals had passed a law in 1871 banning even peaceful protests during strikes. Many working-class men, given the vote in 1867 by the Conservatives, voted for Disraeli in 1875 in revenge. In gratitude, the Conservatives allowed workers to protest peacefully when on strike.

1875 Public Health Act

This Act forced local councils to make health inspections and to improve drains and sewers. This law mostly brought together in one new law all the old laws that had already been passed. It would probably have been passed anyway, whether the Conservatives or the Liberals were in power.

1875 Climbing Boy's Act

This protected children who were forced to work as chimney sweeps. Sometimes the children got buried, suffocated or even jammed in a chimney. A chimney sweep now had to get a licence to work. If he employed children the licence was taken away. This law worked and helped many children. However, the most famous factory reformer, Lord Shaftesbury, supported it. So it would probably have happened anyway, whether the Conservatives or the Liberals were in power.

Think

● What do you think Disraeli meant by 'the lasting affection of the working classes'?

● Which of the laws on page 80, might have **pleased** the working classes the most?

Write a heading: <u>Disraeli's record (2)</u>

Underneath it copy this sentence:
Disraeli said that his first thought was 'the health of the people'.

Now you must judge whether he achieved this or not. Draw two columns as before:

<u>Success</u>	<u>Failure</u>

Choose facts and ideas from page 80 to go into each column.

Upholding the British Empire?

Disraeli said:

The people of England, and especially the working classes of England, are proud of belonging to a great country. There is another aim of the Tory Party – to uphold the Empire of England.

Disraeli encouraged this pride and tried his best to expand the British Empire. During Disraeli's time as Prime Minister, this popular song celebrated the new pride in the Empire:

We don't want to fight
But by jingo if we do,
We've got the ships,
We've got the men,
We've got the money too!

81

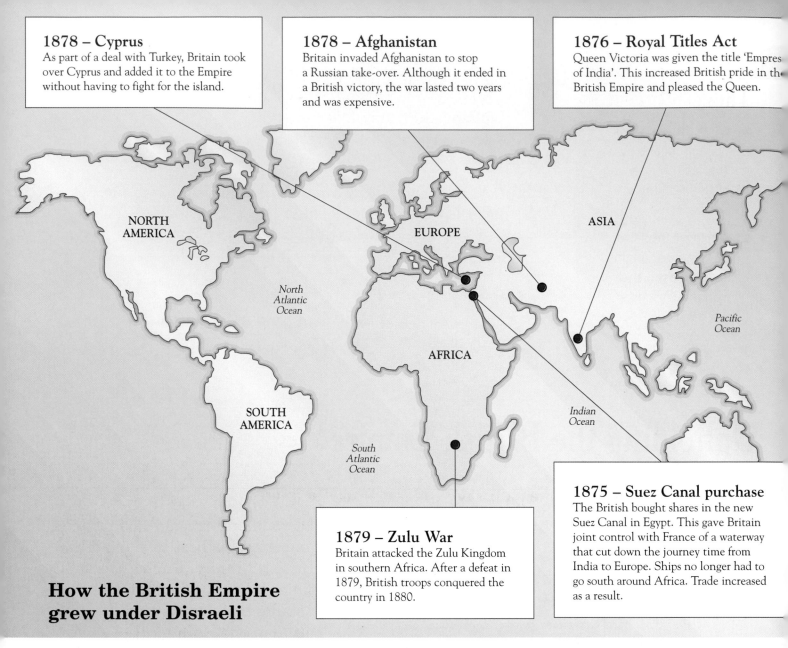

1878 – Cyprus
As part of a deal with Turkey, Britain took over Cyprus and added it to the Empire without having to fight for the island.

1878 – Afghanistan
Britain invaded Afghanistan to stop a Russian take-over. Although it ended in a British victory, the war lasted two years and was expensive.

1876 – Royal Titles Act
Queen Victoria was given the title 'Empress of India'. This increased British pride in the British Empire and pleased the Queen.

NORTH AMERICA

EUROPE

ASIA

North Atlantic Ocean

Pacific Ocean

AFRICA

Indian Ocean

SOUTH AMERICA

South Atlantic Ocean

1879 – Zulu War
Britain attacked the Zulu Kingdom in southern Africa. After a defeat in 1879, British troops conquered the country in 1880.

1875 – Suez Canal purchase
The British bought shares in the new Suez Canal in Egypt. This gave Britain joint control with France of a waterway that cut down the journey time from India to Europe. Ships no longer had to go south around Africa. Trade increased as a result.

How the British Empire grew under Disraeli

On a cold night in Scotland, during the general election of 1880, the Liberal leader, William Gladstone, made a speech to a hall packed with people. At this time, Britain was involved in two costly wars in South Africa and Afghanistan. Gladstone thought this was wrong. He attacked the Prime Minister, Disraeli, saying:

Go from South Africa to the mountains of central Asia. Go into the lofty hills of Afghanistan and what do we see there? Villages burned, women and children driven forth to perish … in the name of England.

Disraeli lost the election to Gladstone. This was partly because the wars in Afghanistan and South Africa were going badly at the time.

Write a heading: <u>Disraeli's record (3)</u>

Underneath it copy this sentence: Disraeli said the Conservative Party should 'uphold the Empire of England'.

Now you must judge whether he achieved this or not. Draw two columns as before:

Success	Failure

By referring to what Disraeli did to expand the British Empire between 1874 and 1880 (pages 81–82), choose facts and ideas to go into each column.

Thinking your enquiry through

You are now ready to write an essay. **Either** use the writing frame below to help you write your essay, remembering to complete each paragraph with several sentences, **or** use a different plan of your own.

However, if you use a plan of your own, you **must** remember to start each paragraph with a main or **big** point. Then use the rest of the paragraph to go into the details (or little points) that support your main idea. Do not use subheadings. This is an essay! For your details, look back at your answers to the three STEPs.

<u>Was Disraeli a failure?</u>

Benjamin Disraeli was Prime Minister twice, firstly in 1868 and again between 1874 and 1880. He often set out his aims very clearly. For example, he said …

(Now finish the paragraph with examples of the hopes and plans that Disraeli spoke about. Use parts of the quotations on pages 78, 80 and 81.)

Disraeli was successful in some ways. He …

However, Disraeli was a failure in other ways. He …

Overall, he was a success/failure. This is because …

'A policy of sewage'

Why did the politicians pass the Public Health Act in 1875?

'The Silent Highwayman' from Punch magazine, 1858

The summer of 1858 was exceptionally hot. There had not been much rain. Sewage could not flow away down the River Thames. The result was the Great Stink. The river smelt so bad that people had to hold handkerchiefs over their faces as they crossed Westminster Bridge. They no longer went on pleasure boats on the river because the paddles stirred up all kinds of terrible filth.

Next to the river, in the Houses of Parliament, the smell was so awful that MPs could no longer do their work. As the cartoon shows, people knew that smell and dirt were linked to disease and death. You might expect the MPs to pass laws to do something about the problem…

…but they did not.

A painting of the Houses of Parliament, 1853

In 1858, the **politicians** at work in the Houses of Parliament shared views like these. They come from *The Times* newspaper in 1854.

> There is nothing a man hates so much as being cleaned against his will, or having his floors swept, his walls whitewashed, his pet dungheaps cleared away. We prefer to take our chance with **cholera** than to be bullied into action.

Think

- According to *The Times*, why would people not like MPs to make new laws to clean up cities like London?

- Which people might disagree with *The Times* newspaper?

Whenever Parliament discussed problems of dirt and disease it seemed to decide that the government should let people get on with their lives without telling them what to do. Then, in 1875, came a clear change. In that year, Parliament debated a Public Health **Act**. This Act would **force** councils to clean up their towns. Here is what the Act said:

- All local authorities **must** appoint a medical officer.
- Local authorities **must** be responsible for sewers, water supplies, rubbish collection, street lighting, public toilets, public parks and checking that food is pure.
- All new houses **must** have piped water and proper toilets, drains and sewers.

In the debate, one MP made fun of the new Act by calling it 'a **policy** of sewage'. He obviously thought Parliament had better things to do – but most MPs now disagreed with him. The Act was passed.

Think

- Which part of the 1875 Public Health Act do you think would be most useful for preventing disease?

- Can you think of any reasons why MPs finally decided to pass this law after so many years of refusing to act?

Your enquiry

Historians often ask why politicians made a particular change at a particular time. In this enquiry you will take the part of an MP. Several different forces were at work, driving you to believe that a Public Health Act must be passed in 1875 after years of delay. You will be searching for arguments and supporting facts to make a short speech persuading other MPs that you are right.

Growing knowledge

One reason why the Public Health Act was passed in 1875 was that people knew much more about the problems of dirt and disease by then.

The Industrial Revolution brought thousands of people into the crowded towns and cities in search of work. Since the 1830s, **Edwin Chadwick**, a **civil servant**, had been gathering facts and figures about life in the cities. He recorded who lived in each house and the age at which they died. He was helped by a new law in 1836. This said that all births, marriages and deaths had to be registered.

Chadwick brought out his famous report in 1842. It showed that British cities faced serious problems. So, in 1843, the Prime Minister, Robert Peel, set up a royal commission to find out about water supplies in 50 large towns. Here are a few of its main findings.

A print of Edwin Chadwick, 1846

- Six towns had good water supplies.
- Thirteen towns had poor water supplies.
- Thirty-one towns had dirty water or not enough water.

Another man who helped to build up useful knowledge about dirt and disease was William Farr. He brought in a system for recording details about how each person in any district died. By the 1850s he and others could use these facts and Chadwick's report to **prove** that disease was far worse where water and sewage systems were bad.

Chadwick and many others believed that dirt poisoned the air and that people fell ill when they breathed in foul smells. In 1854, a brilliant doctor called John Snow showed that a deadly disease called cholera was spread in water not air.

Snow noticed that more people were dying of cholera in the Broad Street area of London than in any other place. He found out that all those who died had drunk water from the same pump. He removed the handle from the pump so that people could not get water there. The outbreak of cholera stopped. His theory was right: **dirty water could kill!**.

Think

- How did John Snow show that cholera was spread in water?

- How could the facts and figures provided by Chadwick and Farr help to save lives?

It seemed that there was a link between dirt and disease – but no one knew exactly what it was!

It was science that provided an answer.

For two hundred years or so, science had been developing new knowledge and new skills. By 1860 a French chemist called **Louis Pasteur** was investigating germs. Germs are tiny micro-organisms which are carried in the air, in water, in dirt, in sewage and in people's spit.

In 1864, Pasteur did an experiment in public which **proved** that germs cause water and other substances to go bad. In 1866, Pasteur proved that a germ caused a disease in silk worms. In Germany, a doctor called Robert Koch found a way of identifying which germ caused which disease. By 1875 these two men were on the edge of proving that germs cause many human diseases.

At first, many people did not believe Pasteur, Koch and their supporters. Even Chadwick hung onto the belief that disease was caused by foul air until he died in 1890.

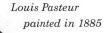

Louis Pasteur painted in 1885

So did the famous nurse, Florence Nightingale. But more and more people were sure that germs caused human disease.

One awful accident in 1866 helped to convince people: the London Water Company accidentally allowed sewage from a district where cholera was already raging to get into the water supply of other areas. Within a few weeks, 7,000 people had died from cholera in London's East End. This was an awful reminder of what Pasteur and others had claimed: **germs cause disease** and germs thrive in dirt and in filthy water. Cleaning up the towns was the only way to stop needless disease.

Think

- What signs can you see in the picture that Pasteur is working scientifically?

STEP 1

Imagine you are an MP in 1875. The House of Commons is discussing whether it should pass the new Public Health Act. You want to make a speech to persuade other MPs that they should pass the act. The speech will have to be quick but full of good ideas and accurate information.

Look through the section called 'Growing knowledge' (pages 86–87). Write down **five key facts** which you will use in your speech to show that new knowledge exists about dirt and disease.

Growing fears

Another reason why the Public Health Act was passed in 1875 was that people were more and more frightened by disease.

Horrible illnesses such as tuberculosis and typhoid killed thousands of poor people in the cities each year. By 1830, people had grown used to these and seemed to accept that they were part of modern life.

Then Britain was struck by a new killer disease: cholera. Cholera reached Britain from India. Here is how it killed its victims:

 1 Start to vomit and have diarrhoea.

 2 Body turns blue-black.

 3 Eyes sink into the head.

 4 Skin goes cold.

 5 Difficult to breathe.

 6 Dies.

There were serious outbreaks of cholera in Britain in 1831–32, in 1848–49, 1853–54 and in 1865–66. Each time it killed thousands of people. No one could ignore this disease – especially because it killed rich and poor alike.

Rich people were often safe from the diseases carried in dirt because their houses were usually cleaner and were in the healthier parts of town. But when cholera broke out it frightened the rich. It seemed to spread so quickly. People who believed the disease was spread through the air were suddenly keen to clear up the slum areas of the towns and cities before cholera spread out to the richer neighbourhoods.

Quite apart from deaths caused by cholera, there were signs that the rich could not always be sure of escaping other diseases which spread from filth. In 1861, Queen Victoria's husband, Prince Albert, died of typhoid. He probably caught the disease from the awful sewers at Windsor Castle.

There was also a fear of a different kind: business men were scared that other countries were catching up on Britain's wealth. Britain needed a healthy workforce if she was to stay ahead of France and Germany.

STEP 2

Continue planning your speech by adding to the notes you began in STEP 1. This time write down **three key facts** from this page which you will use in the speech to show that fear about disease was growing by 1875.

Growing power

A third reason why the politicians passed the Public Health Act in 1875 was that there had been some important changes in who held power and how that power was used.

For most of the 19th century people were expected to look after themselves. This was a strong idea in one of the best-selling books of Victorian times. It was called 'Self Help' and it was written by Samuel Smiles.

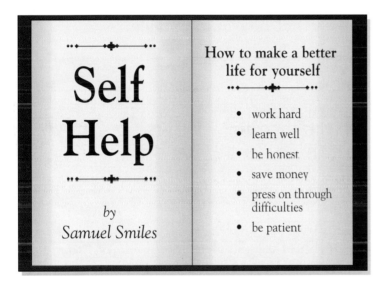

Self Help

by Samuel Smiles

How to make a better life for yourself

- work hard
- learn well
- be honest
- save money
- press on through difficulties
- be patient

Think

- How helpful do you think this advice would be to a poor person?

For most of the 19th century the richer people controlled the government. They believed that Parliament should interfere as little as possible in people's lives. It should leave people to look after themselves. They called this *laissez-faire*.

Most rich voters told their MPs that the country should never pass laws forcing town councils to clean away filth and sewage. They had two reasons for this.

- They feared that new laws would mean that their taxes and rates would go up to pay for drains and water pipes.
- They believed that if the poor were looked after by the tax-payers, then they would never stand on their own feet and look after themselves.

Think

- What is meant by *laissez-faire?*
- Governments today do much more to help the poor than they did in Victorian times. Think of as many examples as you can.

These ideas changed slowly at first. After the cholera outbreak of 1848, Parliament passed several Acts which encouraged towns and cities to supply clean water and to improve drainage. But the Acts **did not force them** to take action. Victorian towns were proud of running their own affairs and they did not want to be ordered about by the government. Cities such as Liverpool, London and Manchester made some improvements but most towns only did something when cholera came. They ignored the problem the rest of the time.

A great change came in 1867.

Before 1867

After 1867

In that year Parliament passed a Reform Act which gave working-class men in the towns and cities the right to vote for MPs and for town **councillors**. Until this time only wealthy men could vote. Parliament and town councils usually tried to please the rich and ignored what the poorer people wanted them to do. The 1867 Reform Act changed that for ever. Now MPs and town councillors would have to please the poorer voters.

The Conservative Party was in power when the Reform Act was passed in 1867. One of the Conservative leaders was Benjamin Disraeli. In 1874, he was Prime Minister. He was determined to win the support of the new working-class voters. In 1872, he made a speech in Manchester. Manchester was one of the biggest and

dirtiest cities in Britain. He promised voters that he would provide:

> Pure air, pure water and the inspection of unhealthy houses. It is impossible to overrate the importance of these subjects. After all, the first consideration of a Minister should be the health of the people.

Benjamin Disraeli

For years most MPs had ignored public health problems. Now the Prime Minister himself was saying that nothing was more important! Disraeli had promised to help. In 1875 he put his Public Health Act before Parliament.

STEP 3

Choose **three key facts** from the section called 'Growing power' (pages 89–90) to show how ideas about power were changing. You will be able to use these in your speech to persuade Parliament that the Public Health Act must be passed.

Thinking your enquiry through

This picture shows the House of Commons. The speech bubbles come from MPs who do not want the Public Health Act to be passed. Imagine you are sitting opposite them. You **do** want the Act to be passed and you want to show that it must be passed now!

Make a short speech which answers all their complaints. Use the list of key facts that you made in STEPs 1, 2 and 3 to help you.

'The most dangerous man in England'

What made Charles Darwin such a threat to people's beliefs?

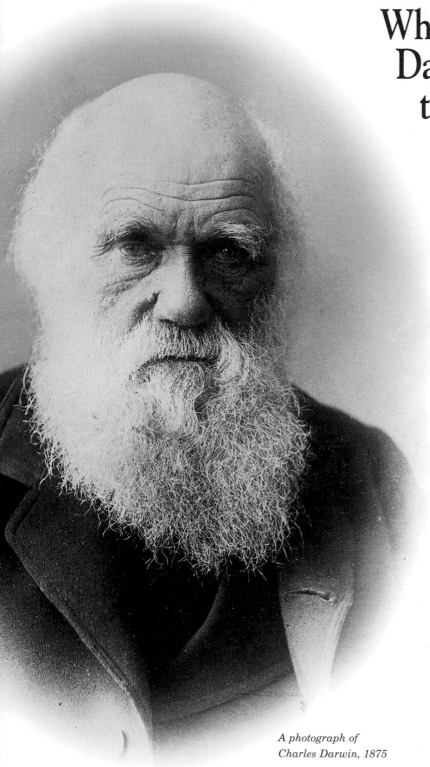

One day in December 1859, an English clergyman was walking with a friend through the British Library in London. Suddenly he stopped and pointed to a large man with a bushy beard who was working quietly at a desk … 'Look!' he whispered to his friend, 'There you see the most dangerous man in England.'

The man he was pointing to was Charles Darwin. This photograph shows you what the 'dangerous man' looked like.

A photograph of Charles Darwin, 1875

Your enquiry

Darwin wasn't a thief or a murderer or a terrorist. He was a naturalist. He wrote books about nature. But the clergyman in the library still thought Darwin was a threat to everything that mattered most to many Victorians. In this enquiry you will learn what was so shocking about Darwin's ideas by putting yourself in the place of a man who knew him well, Robert FitzRoy.

The voyage of the Beagle

On 27 December 1831, a small ship called HMS Beagle left Plymouth harbour. The ship's captain was Robert FitzRoy. He was sailing to South America to make detailed maps of the coast. Sharing his cabin was the young Charles Darwin. FitzRoy had invited Darwin to join the voyage as a naturalist. Darwin was to gather information about the animals, plants and rocks he saw wherever the ship took him.

Darwin was not one of the crew. He was FitzRoy's guest. Being a sea captain was often a lonely job. FitzRoy had decided to find an educated companion to join the voyage.

Darwin had just left Cambridge University and was expecting to become a vicar. But he had always been interested in nature. When he heard that FitzRoy wanted someone to join him he was keen to go. He expected to enter the Church when the voyage was over. But by then his whole life had changed.

Captain Robert FitzRoy

Think

- What job was Darwin expecting to do when he left Cambridge University?

- Why was Darwin keen to join the voyage?

- Why do you think the captain would be more lonely than other crew members on a long sea voyage?

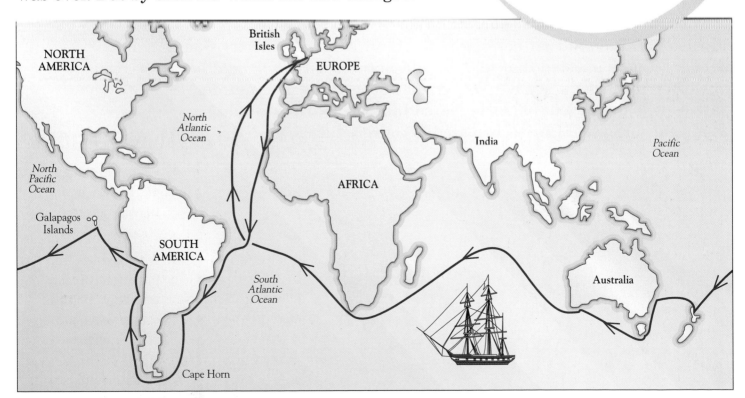

Map showing the route taken by the Beagle

FitzRoy was deeply religious. He wanted Darwin to use his study of nature to show that God really had created every type of creature in just six days. This was what the Church had taught people for over a thousand years.

Darwin agreed with FitzRoy. He believed that the Bible story of **creation** was completely true. But by 1830 several scientists had studied rocks and fossils and said that the world had taken many thousands of years to develop. They used a new word for this long, gradual change. They called it **evolution**. FitzRoy was sure that Darwin could prove that these people were wrong – and Darwin was happy to help.

Decide which of these hopes and expectations FitzRoy **would** have had when the voyage started. Copy them under the heading:

<u>What FitzRoy hoped in 1830</u>

I hope that Darwin will leave me alone.

I hope that Darwin will be good company.

I hope that Darwin will be able to show that the Bible is true.

I hope that Darwin will convince everyone that the idea of evolution is wrong.

I hope that Darwin will make some new discoveries about the world of nature.

New ideas in the New World

As the voyage went on Darwin's friendship with FitzRoy fell apart. They often argued. Darwin hated the slavery he saw in the New World. However, FitzRoy assured him that the slaves were happy. He also told Darwin that nothing in the Bible said that slavery was wrong. FitzRoy insisted that the South American natives should be converted to Christianity, but Darwin had seen white men murder natives who disobeyed them. He feared that whole tribes would disappear for ever if Christians tried to convert them.

Think

● What two things did FitzRoy and Darwin disagree about?

● What signs were there that Darwin was beginning to change his mind about Christianity?

A print of native South Americans, 1830

Darwin and FitzRoy also began to argue about the way the earth had been made. Darwin's beliefs were changing. He could no longer accept the Bible story of creation which said that the world was made in six days. Wherever he went in South America, he found powerful clues that life on earth had been developing over many thousands of years.

Clue 1

He found complete skeletons of creatures which no longer walked the earth. He wondered whether they had died out completely or whether they had changed, over thousands of years, into the creatures he saw on his visit.

Clue 2

Darwin also found fossils of sea shells high up in the Andes mountains! This puzzled him greatly until he visited a town where there had recently been a violent earthquake. Darwin noticed that the earthquake had pushed the land up out of the sea. Maybe this was how the sea shells had appeared in the mountains – but it must have taken thousands of years for them to be lifted so high. Perhaps evolution was true after all?

Clue 3

When Darwin visited the Galapagos Islands in the Pacific Ocean he saw something else which he found strange. He noticed how animals such as the huge tortoises were slightly different on each island. He guessed that they had started off the same but had changed over thousands of years according to the conditions on the island where they lived. It seemed to be another clue that God had not made every type of creature in the first six days.

FitzRoy told Darwin that the extinct animals had obviously not managed to climb aboard Noah's Ark at the time of the Flood. He also claimed that God put the sea shells high in the mountains to test people's faith in Him. Darwin was not convinced. On 2 October 1836, when the Beagle finally reached England again, his doubts were still growing.

STEP 2

Copy and fill a table like this one to show how FitzRoy and Darwin disagreed about some important ideas.

How FitzRoy and Darwin disagreed by 1836

	FitzRoy thought ...	Darwin thought ...
Slavery		
Christianity		
Creation		

The Great Debate

When he returned to England, Darwin decided not to become a vicar. He married and settled down and continued his studies as a naturalist.

Darwin finally published his ideas in *The Origin of Species* in 1859. This was the book which made Darwin seem so dangerous to many Victorians. Earlier writers about evolution had said that the world was not made in six days but they had agreed that someone or something was controlling the changes. Christians could still claim that it was God who was in charge.

But Darwin was different. He dared to say that new creatures developed more or less by accident. He argued that animals were always adapting and changing to suit the world around them. He called this 'natural selection'. If Darwin was right then it seemed that all animals – including man – had developed without any help from God. The Bible said that Adam and Eve were specially made by God, but Darwin seemed to suggest that man was just a well-developed ape! If this was true, then there was no reason why man should obey God or the Church.

Think

- What was the title of Darwin's book?

- Why were Darwin's ideas about evolution more shocking than other people's ideas?

Darwin's book shocked the Church. In 1860, a famous debate took place in Oxford between Bishop Samuel Wilberforce and one of Darwin's supporters, T. H. Huxley.

A cartoon of Bishop Samuel Wilberforce drawn soon after the debate in Oxford

A cartoon of T. H. Huxley drawn soon after the debate in Oxford

The debate ended in uproar. As the audience shook their fists and argued, a small, grey-haired man got to his feet. His face was full of anger and he waved a Bible above his head, shouting 'The Book, The Book!' It was Robert FitzRoy, who had been the captain of the Beagle. He seemed to be showing the fury of millions of Victorians that Darwin had dared to challenge the Bible.

That fury continued long after the debate in Oxford had ended. A few years later, in 1865, poor Robert FitzRoy ended his life by cutting his own throat. Maybe the attack on his faith had helped to drive him to commit suicide.

By the time Darwin died in 1882 millions of people believed that God did not exist, although Darwin himself never agreed with them. Most churches were still well attended on Sundays, but more and more people believed that science had disproved Christianity. People still argue about this today.

STEP 3

Write a short paragraph to explain why FitzRoy was so furious. You must use all these words somewhere in your paragraph:

The Origin of Species	accident
shocking	old
new	six days
evolution	God

Thinking your enquiry through

Imagine you are Robert FitzRoy in 1860. You have been very disturbed by the debate between Bishop Samuel Wilberforce and T. H. Huxley in 1860.

You have decided to write a short pamphlet to warn Victorian church-goers about Darwin's ideas. You decide to divide the leaflet into these four sections:

Why I asked Darwin to join the Beagle in 1831

Why I argued with Darwin on the voyage

What upsets me about Darwin's book, The Origin of Species

Why Darwin is the most dangerous man in England

Write your leaflet. Make sure you show the church-goers how strongly you feel.

Experiences of Empire

How different were the attitudes of the rulers and the ruled?

This cartoon appeared in *Punch* magazine in 1887. The lion represents the people of Britain who were celebrating Queen Victoria's 50 years on the throne. The British were proud that they had been building a huge world-wide **empire** while she was queen.

In Victoria's reign, the British Empire had grown and prospered. But it had not always been like this. Just over a hundred years earlier, the Empire was much smaller. Its most valuable land was in North America.

Think

● What is the lion proud of?

● How has the cartoonist made the British lion look proud?

British people had been settling in North America since 1607. They took land from the Native Americans and started farms and businesses. At first, these **colonists** were quite happy to be ruled from London by the British king and Parliament. But by 1775 many of the colonists were angry. They had to pay taxes to Britain but they were not allowed to have any MPs to speak for them in Parliament. New laws from London interfered with the way the colonists traded. It seemed so unfair!

In 1775, the quarrel between the colonists and King George III turned into open war. The leader of the colonists' army was George Washington. By 1783 Washington's army had beaten the British. The colonies won their freedom from British control and joined together to make the United States of America. The Americans proudly elected George Washington as the first President of their confident new nation. The British were stunned: some feared that the power of their empire had been toppled for ever.

Citizens of New York topple a statue of King George III in 1776, painted in 1854

Your enquiry

Despite losing its American colonies in 1783, the British Empire recovered so well that by 1900 it had grown to be the largest the world had ever seen. No wonder the British lion looked so proud!

However, not everyone was so pleased. In this enquiry you will plan a television series about the different experiences of the rulers and the ruled all over the British Empire.

Think

- Why were the colonists angry by 1775?

- Why are the colonists in the picture toppling the statue?

- Why do you think the Americans chose George Washington as their first President?

The rulers

This map shows the British Empire in 1900. Around the edges you can read about some of the people who helped to make the Empire. These people really existed but they never spoke these exact words. We have researched their lives and we have tried to **imagine** what they would tell us if they were to come back from the dead. Some of their ideas and actions seem shocking to us today.

James McLeod (1836–1894)

"I was a policeman. My father was a British army officer but I was raised in Canada. I joined the Mounted Police – the Mounties – in 1873. We Mounties were proud of the way we treated the natives, or Indians as we called them.
In the United States of America thousands of white soldiers were killed in wars with the Indians. In Canada it was different: hardly a single Mountie was killed by an Indian. We gave them good land to live on, as well as tools and animals and teachers if they wanted them. I am proud of the way the British Empire treated the natives well in Canada."

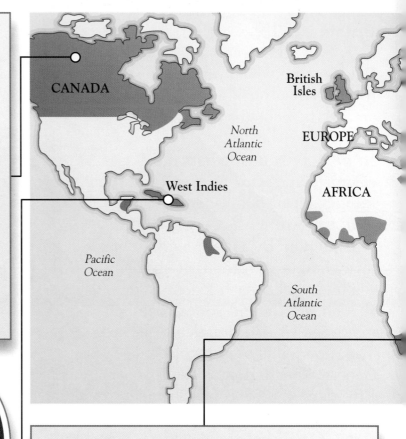

CANADA

British Isles

North Atlantic Ocean

EUROPE

West Indies

AFRICA

Pacific Ocean

South Atlantic Ocean

William Beckford (1709–1770)

"I was a merchant. I was born in Jamaica in the West Indies. My family owned huge sugar plantations there. We bought black slaves from Africa and we sold the sugar cane they grew. That is what the Empire was all about: trade and riches! It helped us all: slaves became Christians, worked hard and were sure of a home and food. Planters became rich. I was a millionaire. I moved back to England and increased my fortune by trading from London."

Cecil Rhodes (1853–1902)

"I was a businessman and politician. I left England to live in southern Africa in 1870. I made a fortune by mining for gold and diamonds. But that was not enough for me: I wanted to change history. We British were the best people in the world so I wanted us to control as much of the world as possible! I made a mining deal with an African chief. When his tribe rose up against my men we crushed them and took their lands. From that time on a new nation was born. It was called Rhodesia. I was proud to have part of the mighty British Empire named after me."

Lord Dalhousie (1806–1857)

"I was Governor-General of India from 1848 to 1856. The East India Company had been taking land there for nearly two hundred years but the English traders did little to improve the way the Indians lived. I worked hard to help the Indians to follow our way of life. I took over land where Indian princes ruled badly. I built roads and railways as well as setting up schools and postal systems. I tried to stop the cruel Indian custom of 'suttee' which said that widows should burn themselves to death on the funeral bonfire of their dead husbands."

Mrs Mary Calvert (died in 1882)

"I was a **missionary**. I sailed with my husband James to the islands of Fiji in 1838. The poor, wretched natives there did not even know about Our Lord Jesus! They had such cruel customs: if a man stole something his children's fingers were cut off. Women were strangled as soon as their husbands died. We did our duty to God and worked with the natives for years. May God be praised, thousands of natives became Christians and gave up their terrible ways."

Edward Gibbon Wakefield (1796–1862)

"I was a thinker and a writer. In 1829, I was in prison in London for tricking a rich woman into marrying me. While in prison I wrote a book which said that Britain should encourage good, honest people to settle in Australia. Until then we had just been sending ship-loads of convicts there. I said young, keen, farming families could use the land properly, improve the country and trade with Britain. My ideas caught on and thousands of British people moved to Australia, New Zealand and Canada."

Pacific Ocean

India

Fiji

Australia

New Zealand

The British Empire in 1900

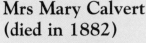

STEP 1

You have been asked to plan a television series about the British Empire. The top line of this chart shows the main theme of each of the five programmes. Copy the chart.

Decide which people might be mentioned in each programme and write their names in the correct column. Some names will go in more than one column.

Money and Empire	Women and Empire	War and Empire	Religion and Empire	Rulers and Empire

The ruled

Here is the same map of the empire in 1900. This time it is surrounded by words from some real people who were ruled over by the British. Once again we have researched their lives and we have tried to **imagine** what they would tell us if they were to come back from the dead.

Rani Lakshmi (died in 1858)

Chief Crowfoot

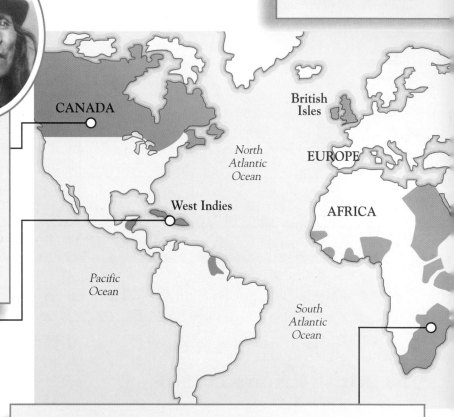

"I was the chief of a tribe in Canada. In 1876, Chief Sitting Bull crossed the border from the United States of America into Canada. He tried to persuade me to join him in a war against the whites. His warriors had just killed General Custer's United States army in a bloody battle. I refused to help Sitting Bull. The Great Mother, Queen Victoria, sent me a message of thanks. I stopped my people rebelling when the railway crossed our land. For this, I was given a life pass on the railway! But since my time the railway has opened up our lands, the number of whites has grown and grown – and very few of my people remain."

CANADA

North Atlantic Ocean

British Isles

EUROPE

West Indies

AFRICA

Pacific Ocean

South Atlantic Ocean

Mary Prince (born in 1788)

"I was born in the West Indies just like William Beckford. But I wasn't a millionaire – I was a poor slave. My ancestors were taken to the West Indies from Africa. I was sold several times and worked for different masters. Some whipped me and others did things so awful that I prefer not talk about them. In 1828, my master took me to London as a maid but I walked out on him. The Anti Slavery Society told my story in a book in 1831. Two years later the British Parliament ended slavery in the Empire – but blacks like me still had the worst jobs."

Chief Lobengula (died in 1894)

"I was the chief of the Matabele tribe in Africa. The whites came during the 1880s and asked to dig for gold on my land. They gave me tools and guns and I allowed them one hole to dig in. Later, I agreed they could dig one more hole in the east. Whites poured onto my land and started mines and farms wherever they liked. I asked the Great White Queen to stop them but she did not. My men bravely stood up to the British who cut them down with their cannons and machine guns. Soon afterwards I died of fever. My people were conquered and our lands were taken."

"I was an Indian princess. I hated the British for taking my husband's land when he died. They ignored our age-old custom which allowed princes to adopt a son to rule after them if they had no children. The British found many ways to interfere with our religion and customs. The Governor-General even upset Indians who were fighting for him in the East India Company army. In 1857, we rose up against the British and tried to drive them out of India. We failed, but at least I died in battle. The British punished survivors by firing cannon balls through them at point-blank range."

Chief Cakobau

"I was the greatest chief of Fiji. When the whites came to our islands they changed our lives. Some traders were cheats, but many missionaries treated us well. In 1854, I became a Christian and my people followed my example. We had to change many of our customs. After I became a Christian the wars between tribes on our islands stopped. The missionaries told me that Fiji would be safer if I took it into the British Empire. The British took over in 1874 and I sent Queen Victoria my favourite war club to say thankyou! Before long the British were growing sugar cane and cotton all over our land."

Bessy Cameron (1851–1895)

"I was a teacher. I came from an aborigine family but I went to a school run by white Australians who had followed Edward Gibbon Wakefield's advice to come to this land. I was taught to be a Christian and to forget aborigine beliefs. At first I was happy to follow the ways of white people. Soon I was teaching other aborigine girls how to count, read, sew, cook and wash for white women. My husband taught aborigine boys about gardening and outdoor work. Later I turned against this way of life – why should aborigines only be trained for the lowest jobs of all?"

Pacific Ocean

India

Fiji

Australia

New Zealand

The British Empire in 1900

STEP 2

Write the names of each of the 'ruled' people in the correct column on the chart you began in STEP 1. Remember that each name can go in more than one column.

Thinking your enquiry through

Bad news! The television company has decided to cut your series from five programmes to two – but the company still wants the series to show in a fair way what the empire was like for the British and for the people they ruled over. Look at the chart you made in STEPs 1 and 2. Decide which two programmes you will keep. Write a letter to the television company explaining

- **what the programmes will be about**
- **why you have chosen to keep these two**
- **what problems you will have in making the two programmes fair**
- **what sorts of information you might need to make your programme accurate.**

East meets West

13

How did a clash of cultures lead to Britain's war with China?

In 1841, a fleet of Chinese warships floated outside the port of Canton. A British steamship, the Nemesis, appeared behind them. The Chinese sailors were amazed. They had never seen a ship like this before. It was a paddle steamer armed with deadly weapons. With just one shot, the paddle steamer blew one of the Chinese warships clean out of the water.

The Chinese stood no chance. Their sailors were armed with bows and arrows. Their cannons had been designed over three hundred years before and they sank without being fired. Two hours after the attack began, five hundred Chinese sailors were dead and the British ship sailed through to capture Canton.

Think

- Why did the British win so easily?

- Why do you think the British and Chinese weapons were so different from each other?

The attack at Canton, painted by a British artist in 1841

Your enquiry

You have seen how a British ship destroyed a Chinese fleet in 1841.
In this enquiry you will be working out what was going on in the minds
of the British and the Chinese to cause this war. It may be difficult.
Even professional historians disagree with each other about this!

A nation of shopkeepers

In 1793, Britain was a rich country.
New British factories produced masses
of useful goods such as pots and pans,
cotton cloth, and knives and forks.
They sold these goods to customers
in Britain and all over the world.

British merchants began to believe
that **everyone** wanted to buy their
goods: they expected **everyone** to
cook with British pots and pans, to wear
British cotton cloth, and to eat with
British knives and forks. The French
Emperor, Napoleon, once said 'The
British are a nation of shopkeepers.'

Think

- What do you think Napoleon's
  comment means?

- How was this comment meant to
  be an insult to the British?

China was a vast and mysterious land
far away from Britain. It was filled
with millions of people – people who
might well become customers for
British traders.

In 1792, the British king, George III, sent
Lord McCartney to discuss trade with the
Chinese emperor. One British cartoonist in
London guessed what it would look like
when McCartney approached the emperor.
Here is his drawing:

Think

- According to the cartoonist, what gifts is
  McCartney bringing to the emperor?

- What does this cartoon tell you about British
  attitudes towards the Chinese in 1792?

McCartney reached China in 1793. When the real meeting took place, he told the emperor of the wonderful goods sold by British traders. The emperor listened carefully but replied by saying:

As you can see, we already have everything we need. We have no use for your country's products. I have always shown the greatest kindness to messengers from kingdoms which long to live as we do. It is your duty to understand my feelings and to obey my instructions for all time.

A Chinese print of the Emperor preparing to receive McCartney in 1793.

The emperor then politely and generously sent gifts to George III. These included silk, jade, books and a pair of slippers. The emperor also gave two cows to Lord McCartney so that he would have a good supply of milk for his English-style tea! But the British visitors were angry and frustrated, and this upset the Chinese.

Think

- Why did the Chinese emperor refuse to trade with Britain?

- Why do you think the British were angry and frustrated?

1 Copy the table below. On each line, tick the box which shows how far you agree with that sentence.

	I agree strongly			I disagree strongly
The British and the Chinese were not getting on well in 1793 because they did not understand each other.	☐	☐	☐	☐
The British and the Chinese were not getting on well in 1793 because they were both proud countries.	☐	☐	☐	☐
The British and the Chinese were not getting on well in 1793 because of trade.	☐	☐	☐	☐

2 Use information from the section 'A nation of shopkeepers' (pages 105–106) to explain your decision for each sentence.

Deadly cargo

What really upset the British traders was that China produced silks, tea and porcelain that would fetch high prices back in Europe. The British had hoped to trade their own pots, pans, knives and forks in exchange for these fine Chinese products – but the Chinese would not let the British goods in. The Chinese government allowed only a few foreign merchants to live in just one port – Canton.

The British were angry that they could not take their goods into China but by 1800 they had found a way round the problem. The answer lay in another part of their empire – India.

Britain had started trading with India around 1600. Since that time most of India had become part of their world-wide empire. From India, British ships took all sorts of valuable goods including one deadly cargo – opium.

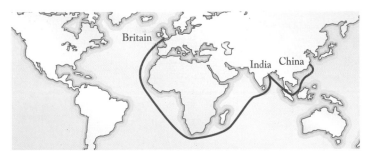

Britain's sea route to India and China

Opium is a drug made from the seeds of the poppy. The Chinese did not want British knives and forks, but **many Chinese did want opium**. British ships carried cargoes of opium from India to China and exchanged them for silk, tea and porcelain.

Between 1800 and 1840 thousands of Chinese people became hooked on opium. They smoked it in pipes in opium dens, even though it ruined their health. The Chinese emperor ordered his people to stop smoking the opium and commanded his officials to stop the British from bringing it into China. But the people took no notice and the officials took British bribes. The trade in opium continued.

In March 1839, a new Chinese official called Lin Tse-hsu arrived in Canton. He was determined to stamp out the opium trade. To the surprise of European traders, he was tough and would take no bribes. He thought Europeans were inferior people. The Chinese called them 'barbarians' – wild and strange people with big, hairy bodies and strangely coloured eyes.

*'Old Hairy One' –
A Chinese impression
of an English sailor*

Think

● Why do you think the Chinese artist made the English sailor look like this?

Lin ordered all European traders to hand over their opium. When they refused, he sealed off the area where the foreigners lived. He also stationed Chinese warships on the river to cut off trade. The Europeans gave in and handed over 28 000 boxes of opium. Lin destroyed all of them. He then demanded that the British end the opium trade completely. Any British ship found carrying opium in Chinese waters would be seized and its officers put to death.

Think

● Imagine you are a British official in London. What would you feel about the Chinese demands?

STEP 2

1 Copy the table below. On each line, tick the box which shows how far you agree with that sentence.

	I agree strongly		I disagree strongly	
The British took advantage of the Chinese by selling them opium.	☐	☐	☐	☐
The Chinese and the British disagreed because Lin Tse-hsu was too tough.	☐	☐	☐	☐

2 Use information from the section 'Deadly cargo' (pages 107–108) to explain your decision for each sentence.

Power and plunder

Back in London, the British Prime Minister, Lord Palmerston, was outraged by the Chinese demands. He ordered a fleet of British warships to launch a attack China.

The Chinese generals were confident that they could beat the British. They called them 'unimportant and hateful'. One of the Chinese generals was over seventy and stone-deaf. He and the other generals believed that simply flying the flag of the Chinese emperor would be enough to make their enemies run away. They were wrong.

Between 1840 and 1842 the British fleet destroyed the Chinese navy and raided the Chinese coast, plundering cities and sometimes attacking ordinary people. The Chinese stood no chance against the guns and modern ships of the Royal Navy. As a result of the British victory. Lin Tse-hsu was sent away in chains. The Chinese had to sign an agreement that was disastrous for them. The treaty said that the Chinese had to:

● pay £2,000,000 towards British war costs

● open up new parts of China to British trade

● leave the opium trade alone

● give the island of Hong Kong to Britain as a base for future trade.

Lord Palmerston was pleased but he did not think much of Hong Kong at the time. He called it a 'barren island'. However it later grew into a massive city and became one of the greatest trading bases of the British Empire.

1 Copy the table below. On each line, tick the box which shows how far you agree with that sentence.

	I agree strongly			I disagree strongly
The Chinese lost the opium war because the British fought unfairly.	☐	☐	☐	☐
The Chinese lost the opium war because they were too proud.	☐	☐	☐	☐

2 Use information from the section 'Power and plunder' (pages 108–109) to explain your decision for each sentence.

Thinking your enquiry through

Historians disagree about why Britain and China went to war.

This paragraph is by a historian called L.C.B. Seaman:

The Chinese behaved with arrogance, ignorance and incompetence. By calling the foreigners barbarians they started the problems. To refuse to treat foreigners as equals and to assume that the foreigners would not be able to defeat them was asking for trouble.

This paragraph is by a historian called Denis Judd:

The opium war was an example of unashamed British aggression. The door to China's trade was smashed through by blatant military intervention.

1 Explain the difference between Seaman's opinion and Judd's opinion.

2 Which historian do you agree with, Seaman or Judd? Use the work you did in STEPs 1, 2 and 3 to help you to give reasons for your answer.

'A citizen of a free country and a woman'

14

Who was Josephine Butler fighting for?

One night in 1864, Josephine and George Butler went out to dinner. They returned late. Their little daughter Eva heard them arrive. She leapt out of bed and ran out onto the landing to greet her parents. In her excitement, Eva ran too fast. Crashing through the banisters, she fell onto the hard, tiled floor of the hall below.

Her father, George, rushed to pick up her up. Later, he wrote in his diary, 'her hair, grown very long lately and of deep chestnut brown which in the sun flashed out all golden … now hung bloodstained and tangled.'

Later that night, Eva died.

This terrible tragedy was a turning point in the life of Eva's mother, Josephine Butler. At first, Josephine's grief was so terrible that she could do nothing. Later, she devoted over twenty years to a long fight for some of the poorest, most disadvantaged women in Victorian Britain. Josephine was trying to change attitudes. She challenged some of the most deeply held beliefs of Victorian people.

Your enquiry

Josephine was a fighter. As you read her story, you will decide who **you** think Josephine Butler was really fighting for. In this enquiry you are going to find out about the different groups of people that Josephine Butler was concerned about and the reasons for her concern. You are going to work out why she was so **significant**.

'My soul's deep discontent'

Josephine was born in Northumberland in 1828. Her father owned thousands of acres of land. Josephine and her sister Hatty spent hours riding their ponies around their father's estates.

Josephine was born into a world of wealth and privilege. It was worlds away from the lives of most ordinary people. This was the life of the upper and upper-middle classes, the privileged few.

Josephine and her five sisters and two brothers all had an excellent education. Their father hired tutors who taught them languages, literature, classics and history. The children took part in discussions and debates. It was unusual for a woman to be educated so well.

Think

- What does 'privilege' mean?

- In what ways was Josephine's life 'privileged'?

- Why do you think that even wealthy women were not usually well educated at this time?

As Josephine grew up she became more and more troubled. She wondered what was the point of her life. She admired her father a great deal and wanted to be like him. She described her father's life as 'a sustained effort for the good of others'. He worked long hours to find new ways of managing his lands and his workers fairly. Josephine wanted to help others, but she did not know how to make herself useful. She felt empty. She wrote about the 'deep discontent' of her soul.

The house where Josephine Butler was brought up

'An interest in a class of sinners'

In 1852, Josephine married George Butler, a tutor at Durham University. George shared Josephine's deep concern to be useful to others. They went to live in Oxford. Together, they planned a future in which they would devote their lives to educating others. They wanted to work for educational **reforms**.

Josephine was happily married. During the first few years of her marriage she was busy bringing up her sons and managing her servants. However, Josephine found living in Oxford difficult. The men who worked with George at Oxford University could not understand Josephine at all!

Photograph of Josephine Butler

Whenever her husband's friends called on the Butlers for tea, Josephine did what most upper-middle class wives did. She looked after her guests by taking charge of the teapot and the stacks of buttered teacakes. But she also did something that most wives did not. When the men's conversation turned to politics or the treatment of women, Josephine **joined in!**

This was shocking. Women of her class were not supposed to talk about sexual matters or politics. These subjects were not 'suitable' for women. George's friends and colleagues did not know how to treat Josephine. They were embarrassed.

They were even more shocked when George allowed his wife to tackle moral problems. When Josephine heard that a young girl was in prison for murdering her baby, she was furious. Everyone knew that the baby's father was a tutor at Balliol College, Oxford. The girl was very poor. Everyone knew that this man had refused to support the girl and her baby.

Josephine went to the Master of Balliol College. She demanded that he challenge the baby's father to take responsibility for the girl. The Master of Balliol College refused to do anything.

Josephine did not give up. She and George gave the girl work as a maid in their own house. This shocked everyone even more. The Master of Balliol College was very disapproving. At the time, he wrote:

> Mrs Butler takes an interest in a class of sinners whom she had better have left to themselves.

Josephine did not see things that way. She was beginning to think that girls like these were not 'sinners' at all. Josephine was starting to think that such girls were

victims.

STEP 1

From the story so far, which of the following groups of people was Josephine concerned about? Choose one of these groups and write down the reasons for your choice:

- working-class women
- all working-class people
- very poor women
- prostitutes
- upper-middle class women
- upper-middle class men
- all women
- all men

Eva

In 1857, George and Josephine moved to Cheltenham. They longed for a daughter. In 1859, Eva was born. For a while, busy with her four children, and sharing in her husband's work, Josephine was fulfilled and happy. Then, in 1864, the terrible tragedy that you read about on page 110 occurred.

Josephine was not able to write about her daughter's death until she was very old. Then she wrote this very upsetting account:

Eva was five-and-a-half, healthy, strong, beautiful, our only daughter. Father and I just adored her, and in a moment she fell, smashed, her head broken, and after hours of awful convulsions she died. For the next 25 years, I never woke from sleep without a vision of Eva's falling figure and without the sound of her head hitting the ground ringing sickeningly in my ears.

'Some pain keener than my own'

Josephine could find nothing to heal her dreadful pain. In 1866, the family moved to Liverpool, but Josephine could not escape from her grief at Eva's death.

It was an old woman, a **Quaker**, who helped her. This woman advised Josephine to lose her own sorrow in other people's. Josephine chose to follow this advice:

> I became possessed with an irresistible desire to go forth and find some pain keener than my own.

Josephine decided to visit workhouses and prisons. She started with Brownlow House where there were over four thousand prostitutes and destitute girls. Victorian people called such girls 'fallen'. They had 'fallen' from goodness into a life of sin. Josephine soon discovered a whole new world of terrible suffering.

Think

- What did Josephine mean by wanting to 'find some pain keener than my own'?

Many middle- and upper-class women visited prisons and workhouses. There was nothing unusual in this. These women saw this work as a religious act. They wanted to help these girls out of their 'wickedness' and to lead them to God. Josephine was religious too, but her approach was different. She listened. She began to learn from the girls' stories.

As Josephine Butler listened to these stories, she soon decided that prostitutes were not wicked. Most of these girls had become prostitutes because of one of two problems:

either

1 They were domestic servants who had become pregnant by a master or son of the household and were then thrown out.

or

2 They were dressmakers or shop girls whose earnings were so small that they needed more money to avoid starvation and homelessness.

Josephine drew two conclusions. The causes of the girls' suffering were:

1 men

2 the economic conditions of the times.

Josephine set about helping these girls in all sorts of ways. She even persuaded some Liverpool merchants to pay for a house where some of the girls could be cared for.

Josephine did not yet know that a much, much bigger project was waiting for her. She was about to begin the great struggle of her life.

From the story so far, which of the following groups of people was Josephine concerned about? Choose one or more of these groups and write down the reasons for your choice:

- working-class women
- all working-class people
- very poor women
- prostitutes
- upper-middle class women
- upper-middle class men
- all women
- all men

'A Parliament of men'

In 1862, Parliament appointed a special committee to find out about the health of the army and navy. MPs were worried about the spread of sexually-transmitted diseases in the armed forces. In the years that followed, three new laws were passed by Parliament. These laws were the Contagious Diseases Acts. They made Josephine Butler very angry. This is what the laws said:

The Contagious Diseases Acts (1864, 1866 and 1869)

- Any woman suspected of being a **prostitute** in ports and army towns has to report to the police station for a medical examination.

- If the medical examination showed that she was diseased then she had to be kept in a locked hospital until she was healthy again.

Think

- Why do you think that these laws made Josephine Butler so angry?

Josephine Butler was so angry that she was beside herself.

She wrote in September 1869:

> Nothing wears me out, body and soul, as anger, fruitless anger … and this thing fills me with such anger, and even hatred, that I fear to face it. The thought of this atrocity kills charity and hinders my prayers.

Josephine Butler was angry for five reasons:

Josephine's first reason

The examinations were not voluntary. Women were held down and inspected with surgical instruments that sometimes caused terrible injury. Josephine believed that these examinations were cruel, brutal and degrading.

Josephine's second reason

All working-class women suffered. Any woman going about the streets in a poor area was likely to be arrested by plain-clothes policemen. All the policeman had to do was suspect that the woman was a prostitute, and he had the power to force her to go for a medical examination.

Josephine's third reason

In Josephine's view, the Acts were punishing the wrong people. Women were seen as 'unclean', but they had not become 'unclean' by themselves! It was men who had given them the disease.

The Contagious Diseases Acts are a good thing. They protect men from unclean women.

Yes! They are an excellent hygienic measure.

Nonsense! The **men** who use prostitutes are also responsible for the spread of the disease. It is **wrong** for men to get off scot-free!

Josephine's fourth reason

Josephine believed that **all women** were wronged by the Acts. If the law treated women's bodies as pieces of meat then **all** women were degraded by it. It cheapened the lives of women. It made it seem as though women were only there for men's pleasure.

Josephine's fifth reason

Josephine was disgusted that the Acts were passed by **men**:

These Acts were passed in a Parliament of men, no woman knowing anything about them. At the very base of the Acts lies the false and poisonous idea that women have nothing to do with the question and ought not to hear of it or meddle with it.

Think

● Why did Josephine believe that prostitutes were wronged by the Acts?

● Why did Josephine believe that all working-class women were wronged by the Acts?

● Why did Josephine believe that **all** women were wronged by the Acts?

STEP 3

From the story so far, which of the following groups of people was Josephine concerned about? Choose one or more of these groups and write down the reasons for your choice:

- working-class women
- all working-class people
- very poor women
- prostitutes
- upper-middle class women
- upper-middle class men
- all women
- all men

'Straight into the jaws of hell'

Josephine set up a Ladies' Association to campaign against the Contagious Diseases Acts. This was a very brave thing to do. Middle- and upper-class Victorian people were shocked at the idea of a woman even using such words as 'sex' or 'prostitute'. She knew she would be publicly criticised and ridiculed.

She was also putting her husband at great risk. Victorian people were shocked that a man could allow his wife to get involved in such matters.

Josephine's aim was the complete **repeal** of the Contagious Diseases Acts. To do this she had to influence MPs and other powerful people. She tried all sorts of methods. Most of them failed miserably.

- She tried writing letters and pamphlets …

  … **but no one took any notice**.

- She gave evidence to a royal commission …

  … **but the men on the commission treated her as though she were making a fuss about nothing**.

- She went on speaking tours, travelling 3,700 miles and attending 99 meetings in the first year alone …

  … **but still no action was taken by the government**.

Josephine had to take more drastic action. She began to interfere in **elections**. This meant that she was no longer speaking to respectable, polite audiences. One of her friends feared that she was going 'straight into the jaws of hell'.

She had to speak on street corners and to face hired gangs of violent trouble-makers. Once, in Pontefract, she had to hide from the mob in a hayloft. The mob set fire to the hay. She only just escaped in time.

Josephine also organised groups of working-class women to resist arrest for being a prostitute. Crowds of furious women would gather around and make it very difficult for a woman to be dragged off for a medical examination. This was very successful. Josephine found huge support.

'The unequal standard in the minds of men'

Josephine also carried on writing. She got better and better at it. She argued not only that **all women** were damaged by the acts, but that **all men** were damaged too. She said that the Acts encouraged men to believed that prostitution was acceptable. They encouraged men to believe that women's bodies were just pieces of meat. This damaged men morally. She said that the Acts 'encouraged in the minds of men the unequal standard that is at the bottom of the whole mischief'.

One of her pamphlets was called *The Constitution Violated*. Here, she said that the rights of individuals living in Britain were under threat. If a person could be dragged off for an examination, without their permission, and without having done anything wrong, then the rights of **all individuals** were under threat. She wrote that she objected to it 'first as a citizen of this country, and then as a woman'.

Think

● What do you think Josephine Butler meant by 'the unequal standard'?

Photograph of Josephine Butler at her desk, reading

STEP 4

From the story so far, which of the following groups of people was Josephine concerned about? Choose one or more of these groups and write down the reasons for your choice:

- working-class women
- all working-class people
- very poor women
- prostitutes
- upper-middle class women
- upper-middle class men
- all women
- all men

'Like a dream'

On the afternoon of 20 April 1881, a week after her 55th birthday, Josephine made her way to the House of Commons to hear yet another Bill to repeal the Contagious Diseases Acts read. By six o'clock, it was clear that the debate would go on all night. So she went to the Westminster Palace Hotel to hold a prayer meeting with her husband, George. At midnight, she returned. As she climbed the stairs to the Ladies' Gallery the steward approached her excitedly. He whispered to her that he thought she was going to win.

He was right. At 1.30am, when the voting figures were called, it was 182 to 110 in favour. Josephine could not believe it. She had worked for 21 years for this moment. She went out onto the terrace of the House of Commons. This is how she felt:

> The fog had cleared away and it was very calm under starlit sky. All the bustle of the city was stilled and the only sound was that of the dark water lapping against the buttresses of the broad stone terrace … It almost seemed like a dream.

From Josephine Butler's diary, 1881

Thinking your enquiry through

So who was Josephine Butler fighting for? Historians like to judge the significance of stories like this. Imagine that you are an historian writing a book about famous women campaigners in the 19th century. Your publisher says that the book is too long and wants to cut your chapter on Josephine Butler. You are furious! Your publisher thinks that other, more famous, women are more important.

You must write to your publisher explaining why you think that the story of Josephine Butler is historically significant. To do this you must convince the publisher that Josephine's fight was much more than a battle for prostitutes. You must explain how and why her struggle was **significant** for other groups of people too.

These sentence-starters may be helpful. You need to find words that will **persuade** your publisher.

Josephine Butler achieved more than …

Josephine Butler cannot be ignored because …

The story of the struggle for women's rights only makes sense if …

I feel strongly that the reader will enjoy this chapter because …

Try to find lots more persuading language of your own!

Victorian pride

15

What can a town's buildings tell us about Victorian minds?

This is Todmorden, a small town on the border between Lancashire and Yorkshire. During the Industrial Revolution the manufacture of cloth moved from the weavers' cottages in the hills around Todmorden to the mills in the valley.

The centre of Todmorden today

Think

- Which things in the photograph of Todmorden today would not have been there in Victorian times?

- Find these Victorian buildings: the town hall, the railway viaduct, the churches, the terraced houses.

In the 19th century, the town became a busy and hard-working place. Many of the mills and the poorer houses have gone, but we can see much of Victorian Todmorden in the buildings which still stand today.

Victorian Todmorden was mainly built with the money of one great family of mill owners – the Fieldens. This statue is a memorial to John Fielden, who died in 1846. It was paid for by the people of Lancashire and Yorkshire who wanted to show their respect and gratitude to John Fielden.

John Fielden's mills provided work for thousands of people in Todmorden. But Fielden was more than a mill owner. As an MP he was one of the most important people behind the 1847 Factory Act. This Act made it illegal for an employer to force anyone under eighteen years of age to work more than ten hours in any one day.

A photograph of John Fielden's statue, 1902

Your enquiry

During the 19th century John Fielden and his three sons, Joshua, Samuel and John (junior), created a thriving cotton business in Todmorden. The brothers did not build good quality houses for their workers as some mill owners did, but the Fieldens did spend part of their great wealth on fine buildings. The Fieldens must have been proud of their town. In this enquiry we will take a careful look at some of Todmorden's Victorian buildings. What can they tell us about the minds of the Victorian mill owners who built them?

Mills and money

A postcard of Lydgate, 1910

Think

- How many storeys has Robinwood Mill?

- How many arches has the railway viaduct?

- Why do you think a picture postcard was made of this scene?

This picture postcard was made in 1910. It shows part of Todmorden called Lydgate. On the right of the picture is Robinwood Mill, one of the Fieldens' cotton-spinning factories. In front of the mill is the dam which supplied the factory with water. In the middle of the postcard you can see the tall arches of the railway viaduct.

John Fielden bought Robinwood Mill in 1843 for £3,900. Over the next ten years the Fieldens spent £34,000 installing steam engines and the latest cotton-spinning machinery. As their business boomed the valley filled with mills. By 1850 the Fielden brothers' business consumed more raw cotton than any other firm in the country. Thousands of Todmorden men and women earnt their living in the Fieldens' spinning and weaving sheds.

John Fielden had always known that his business could grow even faster if one of the new railways could be brought to Todmorden. In 1825, he had helped to form a company which planned to build a railway line between Manchester and Leeds. The line would pass through Todmorden.

Work began on the new railway in 1837. In 1840, the Todmorden section of the line was finally completed. On the opening day the hillsides were crowded with spectators. **They watched in wonder as the first locomotive chugged across the majestic stone arches of the Todmorden railway viaduct.**

Make a table like the one below. Fill in as many details as you can from the information and the photograph in this section.

In the 'Details' column describe what makes the buildings so special. Give dates and other useful background information.

In the 'Fielden pride' column give reasons why the Fieldens wanted these buildings and explain why you think they would have felt proud when the buildings opened.

	Details	Fielden pride
The mills		
The railway		

Faith and hope

The Fieldens, like most Victorians, were deeply religious people. They followed a faith called **Unitarianism**. In 1865, Samuel Fielden laid the foundation stone of this magnificent new Unitarian church in Todmorden.

Samuel and his two brothers built the church in memory of their father. It cost the Fielden brothers £53,000. They employed one of the most talented architects in the country – John Gibson. Gibson's plans for the new building were in the gothic style. The late Victorians loved to copy the architecture of the 12th century.

Gibson gave the church a graceful spire and elegant, pointed windows. He decorated the tower with pinnacles and the walls with buttresses. Inside, the church dazzled with light from the beautiful stained-glass. It took the stonemasons, carpenters and glaziers four years to create this perfect gothic church on the hillside above Todmorden.

A photograph of the Fielden temperance hotel, 1905

Make a table like the one below. Use it to collect information about the Unitarian church and the Fielden temperance hotel.

	Details	Fielden pride
The Unitarian church		
The Fielden temperance hotel		

Think

- Look carefully at the writing above the entrance and work out what the building was used for.

- How has the architect tried to make this building look more important than the other buildings around it?

In 1880, this building was erected in the street below the Unitarian church. You can see who paid for the building from the names on the front!

The building was a **temperance** hotel where no alcohol was served. The Fieldens felt very strongly that drinking alcohol caused crime, poverty and misery. They tried to encourage Todmorden people to drink tea, coffee and chocolate instead.

In the late 19th century many respectable people shared the view that drinking alcohol was wicked. These people often joined Temperance Societies and signed a pledge, promising never to drink. The Fieldens must have been proud of their workers for trying to improve themselves in this way.

Public and private

This is Todmorden town hall. It is the most magnificent building in the town. In 1860, some of the important people in Todmorden formed a company to build a public meeting place with a market underneath. The project soon ran into trouble. In 1865, there was a slump in trade. Money ran out. Building stopped. **You can probably guess who came to the rescue.**

A photograph of Todmorden town hall

You guessed it – the Fieldens!

In 1866, the Fielden brothers bought the half-finished building for £5,500. They employed John Gibson (architect of the Unitarian church) to design a wonderful town hall. The building cost £54,000. It opened in 1875 and in 1891 the Fieldens presented the building to the town of Todmorden.

Think

● Why do you think the Fieldens would have been so proud of the new town hall when it opened in 1875?

● Why do you think some people might say that it was the Fieldens' workers who paid for this building?

The statues on Todmorden town hall

Todmorden town hall is built in the classical style of ancient Greece and Rome. It has elegant columns, arched windows and beautifully carved statues. In those days the building was half in Yorkshire and half in Lancashire. The statues above the entrance show the cotton-spinning of Lancashire and the engineering and farming of Yorkshire.

It would be wrong to think that the Fieldens only spent money on public buildings. The profits from their business made the Fieldens one of the wealthiest families in Yorkshire. They lived in great luxury. This picture shows Dobroyd Castle. It was built by John Fielden (junior) as a new home for himself and his wife, Ruth.

Dobroyd Castle had 66 rooms and cost £72,000 to build – much more than the Fieldens spent on the Unitarian church or the town hall.

A postcard of Dobroyd Castle, made in 1905

Think

● How has the architect (John Gibson again) made the Fieldens' new home look like a medieval castle?

● Why do you think John Fielden wanted his house to look like a medieval castle?

125

Make a table like the one below. Use it to collect information about the town hall and Dobroyd Castle.

	Details	Fielden pride
Town Hall		
Dobroyd Castle		

Thinking your enquiry through

This photograph of John Fielden (junior) was taken outside the door of Dobroyd Castle in about 1890. Some years before, a kick from a horse shattered John Fielden's leg and left him in a wheelchair.

Work in pairs. It is 1890. One of you is a reporter for the *Yorkshire Post* newspaper. You have been sent to Dobroyd Castle to interview John Fielden about his pride in the buildings he and his family have erected in Todmorden. The other is John Fielden.

Use the information in the tables you made in STEPs 1, 2 and 3 to write an interview between the *Yorkshire Post* reporter and John Fielden. Structure your interview around these buildings:

- the mills
- the railway
- the Unitarian church
- the temperance hotel
- the town hall
- Dobroyd Castle

A photograph of John Fielden (junior) outside Dobroyd Castle, 1890

Glossary

abolition Banning something, e.g. slavery

apprentice A young person who is learning a trade

Act A new law passed by Parliament

biased One-sided; not being fair to all sides

Bill The name given to an Act before it is passed by Parliament

cargo Goods carried by ships

Chartist Someone who wanted working-class people to have the right to vote for MPs

charter A list, e.g. of the changes that Chartists wanted

civil servant Someone who works for the government

class A group of people

colonists People who live in colonies, i.e. land taken in another country

commission A group of people who work together on a task for the government

Conservative The political group which usually dislikes making changes to old ways of doing things

councillor A member of a council, e.g. one which runs a town's affairs

creation The Bible story that God made the world in six days

demographic To do with population, i.e. the number of people living in a place

election Choosing a leader by voting

emigrant Someone who leaves one country to go to another

empire A large group of countries ruled by one power

epidemic An outbreak of a disease that spreads very quickly

evangelical Someone who believes it is very important to spread Christian ideas

evolution Change which happens over a long period of time

famine A time of great hunger

industrial To do with industry, i.e. how people make things, especially in factories

Industrial Revolution The time of great change in Britain when people began to make things by machine in factories (c1780–1830)

invest To put money into a business

laissez-faire The belief that governments should leave people to look after themselves

Liberal The political group which usually tries to give individual people as much freedom as possible

Methodist A Christian who follows the ideas of John Wesley

mill A factory

missionary Someone who spreads ideas, e.g. about religion

non-conformist	A Christian who does not belong to the Church of England but who is a Protestant
outdoor relief	Giving money to help poor people who do not live in workhouses
overseer	A person in charge of a group of workers
pauper	A poor person who is being supported by rate-payers' money
plantation	A large farm growing one crop, e.g. sugar, tobacco or cotton
policy	A plan of action
politician	Someone who tries to gain power to help rule a country
poverty	Being poor
prejudice	Unfair opinions that are not based on facts
prostitute	Someone who accepts money in return for having sex with another person
privy	An outside lavatory
Quaker	A type of Christian with a strong belief in peace
radical	Someone who wants to make big changes
rate-payers	People who pay taxes to help run local government
refine	To make something clean and pure, e.g. refined sugar
reform	To change something, making it better
reformer	Someone who wants to make changes

reliable	Someone or something that can be trusted
repeal	To remove a law
revolution	A big and speedy change
riot	A violent disturbance where a crowd of people gets out of control
rural	To do with the countryside
slave	Someone who is owned by another person
temperance	Refusing to drink any form of alcohol
textiles	Cloth, e.g. made from cotton or wool
Tory	The political group which usually dislikes making changes to old ways of doing things
trade union	A group of people who join together to improve their pay or working conditions
transported	Sent away to live in another land
Unitarian	A church group which does not accept that Jesus was equal with God
unreliable	Someone or something that cannot be trusted
urban	To do with towns or cities
Whig	The political group which was usually happy to make some changes to old ways of doing things
workhouse	Place where poor people were given food and shelter in return for work